THE
50
STATES

BUCKET LIST

THE ULTIMATE
JOURNAL FOR
A JOURNEY ACROSS
AMERICA

JESSICA LAUGHLIN

EPIC INK

Contents

Introduction

When I was a kid, taking a trip was a big deal. My parents would plan for months in advance and then we'd count down the days, until the morning finally came when we piled into the car and took off. At some point, we would stop for a big breakfast special, and then, once back in the car, Dad would put on Willie Nelson's "On the Road Again" and we were officially off on whatever journey awaited us.

We'd stop at every landmark along the way, of course. Dad would say proudly, like a tour guide, "Now, we have reached Pea Soup Andersen's—you know, this is the most famous pea soup in the world!" or, "Here we are at the Four Corners, where we can officially be in four states at once!"

All of this is probably where my quirky adoration for maps, and especially roadside atlases began to take form. When you live in Las Vegas, it feels like living on an island, but rather than being surrounded by water, you have desert for miles around. While following the highway lines with my finger, I would look at the atlas and imagine all the places I would eventually visit. Perhaps you had these same experiences growing up, or maybe you are ready to take off on a new adventure of your own.

Today, when my husband and I hit the road, some of the best times we have are the least planned. On the road to Santa Fe last summer, it took us at least twice as long as it should have. The sun-bleached, hand-painted signs from the old Route 66 days beckoned me to stop at least every thirty miles.

Every state has its own unique qualities. The United States of America is amazing in that way. The diversity of landscapes and cultures is incredible, from stunning coastlines to fields of corn, lush green forests to deserts and badlands. Nevada, my home, is an unusual state, with much of its beauty found in its ruggedness, but it also has a softer side of sunsets seemingly painted with brilliant hues of pink. So how can one even begin to highlight all the important things to see? This collection is a starting point, a suggestion from me to you. I hope you add your own list of experiences to it, for your own memories or for someone else to see one day. Your journey and your journal will be one of a kind.

You may think that seeing all fifty states is impossible in a lifetime. Or maybe you're lucky enough to have already seen a good share of them. Either way, there's no shortcut to traveling all fifty states. And even if there was, what fun would that be? When you take the scenic route and cruise in the slow lane, you will experience more of the little things that make this country special. In my opinion, when you take time to travel, it simply enriches your soul.

I have yet to visit all fifty states, but I sure hope that I will get to each one at some point. In the meantime, I hope that you enjoy your journey, have safe travels, and, however old you are, make sure to just have fun and stop along the way.

How to Use This Journal

This journal is meant to record your best travel experiences as you journey through the United States. I have included information about each state's history, culture, and key attractions for your reference. Some of the destinations mentioned are unusual detours, but oftentimes those are the most fun!

While on your adventures, you'll discover your own favorite road-trip stops, scenic routes, and points of interest to add in the journal pages. Plan your trips and document where your journeys lead you with art and prompts, including:

❏ **ILLUSTRATED MAPS** – Each illustrated state map highlights some of that state's landmarks, terrain, wildlife, and culture.

❏ **JUST THE FACTS** – This section is for logistical information for your trip. When looking back years from now, you'll have a record of how you got there, who was with you, and where you stayed.

❏ **LOCAL CUISINE** – When on vacation, it's always fun to try new flavors. Every state has a food that it's known for—like Maine's lobster rolls, Vermont's maple syrup, or Texas' barbecue. Keep track of every local delicacy you try.

❏ **GETTING CULTURED** – The United States is filled with diversity, and that's what makes it unique! Each state offers ways to immerse yourself in different cultures and expand your knowledge through historic sites and museums. Note down some of your favorites in this section.

❏ **FIRST TIME?** – Check off whether it was your first trip to the state or not.

❏ **HAD TO SEE IT TO BELIEVE IT** – America's highways and small towns are known for an eclectic assortment of attractions. Write down some of the strangest or most interesting things you see.

❏ **RATE THE STATE** – Give the states you visit a rating from one to five stars, based on your trip experience. (Hopefully they're all fives!)

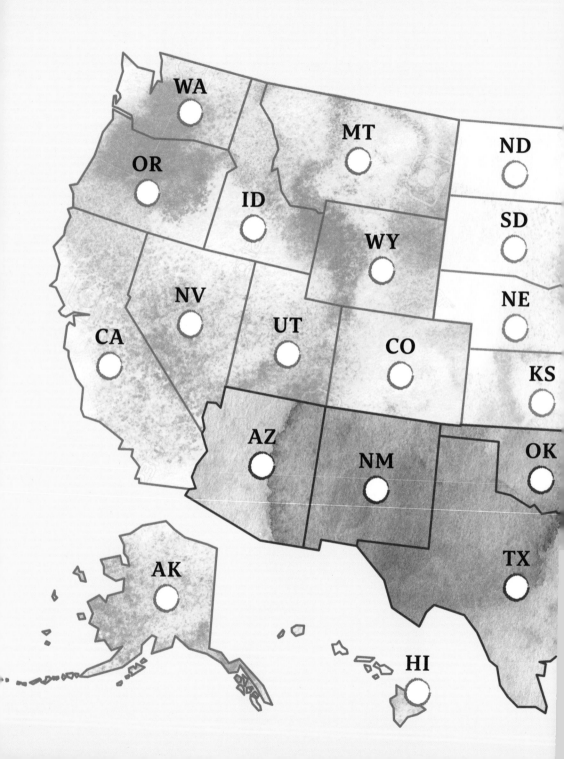

The Land of the Free

Once you've visited a state,
check it off on the map!

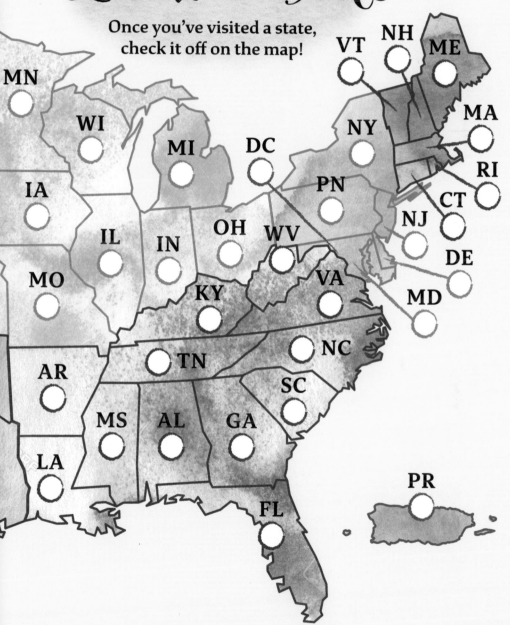

THE
WEST

The West is legendary for its storied history and blended cultures. Though to many it's considered the last frontier, indigenous peoples inhabited the western part of America for centuries. Their ways of life and traditions remain deeply embedded in the spirit of the West. In the early days of our country, pioneers traveling by covered wagons paved the way for the West to expand. The construction of the transcontinental railroad and the discovery of gold in California marked two significant moments that later spurred even more migrations. Our vision of the West still holds onto tales of cowboys, outlaws, boomtowns, wide-open spaces, and surreal landscapes.

Alaska

— est. 1959 —

THE LAST FRONTIER Known as "The Last Frontier," Alaska is the largest and most wide-open state in the country. Indigenous peoples have lived in Alaska for thousands of years and their cultures have greatly influenced the Alaskan way of life. Totem poles, for example, are an important part of Alaskan heritage and can be found in abundance throughout the state (the largest collection is located in Ketchikan). While exploring small fishing villages, natural wonders, and the beautiful scenery, you will see why Alaska is such a special place.

State Capital: **Juneau**
State Flower: **Forget-me-not**
State Bird: **Willow Ptarmigan**
Tallest Mountain: **Denali**

Katmai National Park & Preserve

Visitors come to Katmai from all over the world to see the iconic brown bears catching wild sockeye salmon at Brooks Falls. This sprawling park is just over 4,000,000 acres and contains the world's largest population of protected brown bears. The best time to visit for a chance at a bear sighting is during the summer, from July through early September. Katmai's diverse terrain was in part created by volcanic activity. One of the most notable areas is the Valley of Ten Thousand Smokes, which was formed by the eruption of a new volcano, Novarupta, in Katmai in 1912. The park is a spectacular natural wonder, and though it is very large, most who visit stay at Brooks Camp.

The Northern Lights

The best time of the year to view the Northern Lights is in the winter months. During December and January, some parts of Alaska are in twenty-four-hour darkness. On the flip side, in summer those same places have near constant daylight and for this reason, Alaska has been called, "The Land of the Midnight Sun." This natural phenomenon is known for bright green and yellow auras streaking through the night sky.

Igloos

Historically, the native Inuit people of Alaska lived in igloos during the extremely cold winters. Igloos are made of pressed snow, formed in a dome shape, and are insulated by human body heat. When people gather inside, body heat is contained within the igloo to keep everyone warm.

Did you know? Utqiagvik is the northernmost town in the United States.

Wild & Scenic Alaska

❏ Denali National Park and Preserve
❏ Kenai Fjords National Park
❏ Alaska Wildlife Conservation Center
❏ Wrangell-St. Elias National Park and Preserve

ALASKA

JUST THE FACTS

DATE(S) VISITED

TRAVEL COMPANION(S)

MODE OF TRANSPORTATION

WEATHER

LODGINGS

LOCAL Cuisine

Best state delicacy eaten _____

_____

_____

_____

_____

FIRST TIME?

Was this your first visit, or are you basically a local?

☐ YES   ☐ NO

HAD TO SEE IT TO BELIEVE IT

Strangest tourist attraction visited _____

_____

_____

_____

_____

GETTING CULTURED

Museums or other points of interest visited

RATE THE STATE

☆ ☆ ☆ ☆ ☆

California

— est. 1850 —

THE GOLDEN STATE There are great contrasts in California. Death Valley, the hottest place on the planet, holds a remarkable silence. On the other hand, the sounds of waves and seagulls fill the atmosphere along the coast. When gold was discovered in 1848 on the American River in Coloma, droves of gold-panners arrived with not much more than hope. Decades later, young starlets came to Hollywood with the same enthusiasm. While not all would find fame or nuggets of gold, they all arrived in search of the California Dream.

STATE FACTS

State Capital: **Sacramento**
State Flower: **California Poppy**
State Bird: **California Quail**
Oldest Tree: **Methuselah (Bristlecone Pine)**

Highway 1

California's Pacific Coast Highway trails much of the state's coastline from Mendocino to Orange County and is an ideal way to see several beach towns on one scenic drive. A good jumping-on point is Monterey Bay, where John Steinbeck wrote the classic *Cannery Row* and the Monterey Bay Aquarium gives a magnified view of rare ocean life. After driving over Bixby Bridge, you enter Big Sur, where the twists and turns gain momentum, but so do the sweeping views. Eventually, you reach San Simeon, where Hearst Castle rises among the clouds on its golden hill, and zebras roam the expansive grounds.

The City of Angels

The hillside Hollywood sign has summoned dreamers to Tinseltown since the days of silent films. Walk among the stars on the Hollywood Walk of Fame, make sure to see the glamorous lifestyle of America's most famous zip code (Beverly Hills, 90210), and escape the city traffic for nearby Malibu Beach.

The Heart of San Francisco

It's easy to leave your heart in the fogged-in city by the bay. For over 150 years, cable cars have carried passengers up and down the hills. Make time to visit Lombard Street (the "Crookedest Street in the World"), Haight-Ashbury, the Palace of Fine Arts, Union Square, Powell Street, and the notorious prison on Alcatraz Island.

California Dream Locations

❏ Yosemite National Park
❏ The 17-Mile Drive Lone Cypress
❏ Mid-Century Modern Palm Springs
❏ The Danish village of Solvang
❏ Old Sacramento Waterfront
❏ Wine country of Sonoma and Napa Valleys
❏ Santa Barbara Arts and Crafts Show
❏ Santa Catalina Island
❏ Santa Cruz Beach Boardwalk

CALIFORNIA

JUST THE FACTS

DATE(S)
VISITED

TRAVEL
COMPANION(S)

MODE OF
TRANSPORTATION

WEATHER

LODGINGS

LOCAL *Cuisine*

Best state delicacy eaten _____

GETTING CULTURED

Museums or other points of interest visited

FIRST TIME?

Was this your first visit, or are you basically a local?

YES ☐ NO ☐

HAD TO SEE IT TO BELIEVE IT

Strangest tourist attraction visited _____

RATE THE STATE

☆ ☆ ☆ ☆ ☆

Colorado

— est. 1876 —

THE CENTENNIAL STATE When the snow melts in late June, alpine meadows in Crested Butte come alive with an astounding array of wildflowers bursting in color. Every season in Colorado brings about new miracles of nature. Rocky Mountain peaks, golden aspens, and the rushing rapids of the Colorado River provide infinite inspiration all year through.

State Capital: **Denver**
State Flower: **Rocky Mountain Columbine**
State Bird: **Lark Bunting**
Highest Mountain: **Mount Elbert**

The Rockies

Rocky Mountain National Park, located in the north central region of the state, contains over 60 mountain peaks and is located at one of the highest elevations in the country. The Continental Divide passes through the park, giving way to the striking canyons, valleys, and rivers. Moose dip into the glacial lakes silhouetted by sunlight and bald eagles soar above the summits. Conifer forests provide shelter to bears, mountain lions, and deer. Just two hours outside the "Mile High City" of Denver, this national park is enjoyed by millions of visitors each year, and most stay in Estes Park. It's not uncommon to spot families of elk in this gateway town.

Winter Ski Towns

Summers in Colorado are heavenly, but many people can't wait to hit the slopes in winter. Colorado has amazing skiing and snowboarding, not to mention mountain towns that turn into winter wonderlands. Grab a hot cocoa and get cozy by the fire in a rustic log cabin, or stroll through the snowy downtowns of Telluride, Aspen, Vail, or Breckenridge. Epic days of gliding down the mountain ranges of the Rockies are paired with Colorado's old Western ways during the annual Cowboy Downhill at Steamboat Resort. This event showcases the skills of pro rodeo stars as they compete on the slopes in cowboy hats and skis.

Did you know? Great Sand Dunes National Park and Preserve features the tallest sand dunes in North America, including Star Dune, which stands 750 feet tall.

Into the Rockies and Beyond

- ❏ Mesa Verde National Park
- ❏ Pikes Peak Cog Railway in Manitou Springs
- ❏ Fort Collins' Old Town Square
- ❏ Red Rocks Park and Amphitheater in Morrison
- ❏ Garden of the Gods in Colorado Springs
- ❏ Pagosa Springs

COLORADO

JUST THE FACTS

DATE(S) VISITED

TRAVEL COMPANION(S)

MODE OF TRANSPORTATION

WEATHER

LODGINGS

LOCAL Cuisine

Best state delicacy eaten _____

GETTING CULTURED

Museums or other points of interest visited

FIRST TIME?

Was this your first visit, or are you basically a local?

☐ YES ☐ NO

HAD TO SEE IT TO BELIEVE IT

Strangest tourist attraction visited _____

RATE THE STATE

☆ ☆ ☆ ☆ ☆

Hawaii

— est. 1959 —

THE ALOHA STATE The story of Hawaii is framed by the island's Polynesian lineage. Around 400 AD, the island chain was discovered by people from the Marquesas Islands in the South Pacific, who paddled through the ocean in long canoes. These people developed the land and created new traditions. Passed down by their ancestors, the traditions of hula, luaus, and fire dancing are the fabric of Native Hawaiian culture. There are eight main islands that make up Hawaii—Maui, Kauai, Oahu, Molokai, Lanai, Kahoolawe, Niihau, and the Big Island—but there are also 130 smaller islets and atolls. The brilliant clear waters, breaking waves, and tropical forests make this state America's paradise in the Pacific.

STATE FACTS

State Capital: **Honolulu**
State Flower: **Yellow Hibiscus**
State Bird: **Nene**
Popular Food: **Pineapple**

Beaches of Oahu

Aloha from Hawaii's capital, Honolulu, on the island of Oahu! This densely populated city has a multitude of high-rise resorts just steps from the beach. The crescent-shaped Waikiki Beach is renowned for its clear turquoise water. Diamond Head, an inactive volcano crater, is a prominent mountainous landmark on the far eastern bend of the beach. With the Iolani Palace not far away, Hawaiian royalty would ride the waves among these same tides, as surfing was once the "Sport of Kings." The North Shore, on the opposite side of the island, is the laidback counterpart to Waikiki. Locals catch the breaks of huge waves on Waimea Bay Beach. This northern stretch of Oahu, known for its notorious swells, also hosts surf competitions.

The Road to Hana

The Road to Hana in Maui features miles of sharp turns and dramatic cliffs that showcase panoramic views of the sea. There are turnoffs on the road to sightsee and hike, as well as exits for remote coasts like the exquisite Hamoa Beach. Throughout the drive, there are waterfalls, lagoons, and beaches of red and black sand.

Flavors of Hawaii

Taste the islands with these classic Hawaiian favorites: shave ice, acai bowls, poke, Haupia pie, Kalua pork, poi, grilled pineapple, and the standard Hawaiian "plate lunch," consisting of rice, teriyaki meat, and macaroni salad.

Island Hopping

- ❏ Pearl Harbor National Memorial, Oahu
- ❏ Hawai'i Volcanoes National Park, Hawaii
- ❏ Rainbow Falls in Hilo, Hawaii
- ❏ Kalaupapa National Historical Park, Molokai
- ❏ Hanalei Beach, Kauai
- ❏ Hulopoe Beach, Lanai

NIIHAU

KAUAI

OAHU

MOLOKAI

MAUI

LANAI

PACIFIC
OCEAN

KAHOOLAWE

HAWAII

Hawaii

THE ALOHA STATE

HAWAII

JUST THE FACTS

DATE(S) VISITED

TRAVEL COMPANION(S)

MODE OF TRANSPORTATION

WEATHER

LODGINGS

LOCAL Cuisine

Best state delicacy eaten _____

_____

_____

_____

_____

_____

GETTING CULTURED

Museums or other points of interest visited

_____

_____

_____

_____

_____

_____

_____

FIRST TIME?

Was this your first visit, or are you basically a local?

☐ YES ☐ NO

HAD TO SEE IT TO BELIEVE IT

Strangest tourist attraction visited _____

_____

_____

_____

_____

_____

_____

RATE THE STATE

☆☆☆☆☆

Idaho

— est. 1890 —

THE GEM STATE When thinking about Idaho, the potato certainly comes to mind. Along the Snake River, the flat plains possess a particularly good climate for growing spuds, so Idaho grows the most potatoes in America. Though the southern portion of Idaho is less mountainous, the central region to the northern panhandle has forested river valleys, mountains, and lakes. From these mountain ranges come various precious gemstones. The star garnet received recognition as the state's gemstone for its rarity.

STATE FACTS

State Capital: **Boise**
State Flower: **Syringa**
State Bird: **Mountain Bluebird**
Popular Food: **Huckleberry Pie**

Coeur d'Alene

Coeur d'Alene was established in 1887 on the banks of Coeur d'Alene Lake. From that point forward, it transitioned into a military fort, railroad trading hub, and mining and timber frontier town. The summer months on this glimmering lake enveloped by green hills are breathtaking, and many come just to set sail or fish for salmon and bass. There is also a lot to see in the endearing downtown. Western storefronts and restaurants along Sherman Avenue maintain a touch of their French heritage, with sidewalk cafes, pastry shops serving macarons, and flowers in hanging pots.

The Streets of Boise

Golden hills embrace this capital city located on the banks of the Boise River. Mature trees and open space provide an escape from urban life on the trails of the Boise River Greenbelt. There are ten distinctive historic

districts around the city, making it a great place to spend an afternoon walking. Hyde Park and Old Boise are two of the city's historic centers, whereas one of the most winsome neighborhoods is Harrison Boulevard, known for its maple trees and stately homes.

Sacagawea's Idaho

Sacagawea led Lewis and Clark on their expedition west from North Dakota to the Pacific Coast through native territories. She was born in Idaho, near Salmon Falls, into the Shoshone tribe. The Sacajawea Center in Salmon features a dynamic bronze sculpture of her, holding her baby, with the mountains behind her. This is a primary spot of interest along the Lewis and Clark National Historic Trail that extends from Pittsburg, Pennsylvania, to the Columbia River near Astoria, Oregon.

Idaho Travel Gems

- ❏ Sun Valley
- ❏ Hells Canyon
- ❏ Craters of the Moon National Monument and Preserve
- ❏ Shoshone Falls Park
- ❏ The Idaho Potato Museum in Blackfoot
- ❏ Idaho Falls River Walk

Idaho

THE GEM STATE

COEUR D' ALENE

BOISE ★

SUN VALLEY

IDAHO FALLS

POCATELLO

TWIN FALLS

IDAHO

JUST THE FACTS

DATE(S) VISITED

TRAVEL COMPANION(S)

MODE OF TRANSPORTATION

WEATHER

LODGINGS

LOCAL Cuisine

Best state delicacy eaten _____

GETTING CULTURED

Museums or other points of interest visited

FIRST TIME?

Was this your first visit, or are you basically a local?

☐ YES ☐ NO

HAD TO SEE IT TO BELIEVE IT

Strangest tourist attraction visited _____

RATE THE STATE

☆ ☆ ☆ ☆ ☆

Montana

— est. 1889 —

THE TREASURE STATE Montana is a work of art on Mother Nature's canvas. When spending time in "Big Sky Country," experience the majesty of mountains, rivers, and wide-open ranges during the day, and countless sparkling stars at night. Montana has relatively few tall buildings, leading to an appreciation for its unobstructed skies. Due to this, even the cities of Billings and Missoula feel like small towns. The allure of the western way of life comes true here, as you venture into a state loved for its landscapes and big skies.

On the Rivers

Montana is known for flyfishing, especially in the southern region. Scenes from 1992's *A River Runs Through It* were filmed in the Gallatin Canyon, south of Bozeman. This area may be best accessed off Route 191—follow the river access signage. The Gallatin, Madison, and Jefferson Rivers join in Three Forks, forming the beginning of the Missouri River's journey east to the Mississippi River. Missouri Headwaters State Park marks the start of the Missouri, the longest river in America.

The Crown of the Continent

Going-to-the-Sun Road in Glacier National Park crosses glacier-carved valleys and scales sharp mountainsides. On a clear day, this route's highest elevational point at Logan Pass (6,646 feet high) showcases the enormity of the Continental Divide. Mountain goats don't seem to mind the heights, as they play along the rocky edges. This great alpine ecosystem contains rushing rivers, waterfalls, and over 700 ice-cold lakes. The largest lake, Lake McDonald, is encircled by snow-covered peaks. Bordered by Canada to the north, this stunning national park is the "Crown of the Continent."

Under the Big Skies

- ❏ Missoula's Clark Fork River
- ❏ Fossils at Bozeman's Museum of the Rockies
- ❏ Lewis and Clark Caverns State Park
- ❏ West Yellowstone
- ❏ Great Falls
- ❏ The City of Whitefish

Montana

THE TREASURE STATE

GREAT FALLS

MISSOURI RIVER

MISSOULA

★ HELENA

YELLOWSTONE RIVER

BOZEMAN

● BILLINGS

● WEST YELLOWSTONE

MONTANA

JUST THE FACTS

DATE(S) VISITED

TRAVEL COMPANION(S)

MODE OF TRANSPORTATION

WEATHER

LODGINGS

LOCAL Cuisine

Best state delicacy eaten _____

GETTING CULTURED

Museums or other points of interest visited

FIRST TIME?

Was this your first visit, or are you basically a local?

☐ YES   ☐ NO

HAD TO SEE IT TO BELIEVE IT

Strangest tourist attraction visited _____

RATE THE STATE

☆ ☆ ☆ ☆ ☆

Nevada

— est. 1864 —

THE SILVER STATE Nevada is known as the Silver State for its history in silver mining. In 1859, silver was discovered, which brought thousands of eager prospectors and miners to the state. Nevada is also famous for gold mining. Boomtowns developed throughout the state, many of which flourished for a short time, then were later abandoned. Many "ghost towns" are still standing today throughout Nevada's rugged terrain, as relics of the silver-mining glory days.

STATE FACTS

State Capital: **Carson City**
State Flower: **Sagebrush**
State Bird: **Mountain Bluebird**
Largest Lake: **Lake Mead**

Strange Drives
The Loneliest Road in America. Highway 50 from Carson City to Ely is known for its desolation, so make sure you are prepared for long stretches of wide-open spaces between towns.
The Extraterrestrial Highway. The E.T. Highway 375 passes through an area known as Alien Country, because it's home to the top-secret Area 51.

Las Vegas
The first casinos in Las Vegas were built primarily for the Hoover Dam workers. From this early period, the mafia had great influence in making the city into a tourist destination, and this continued throughout most of the twentieth century. Fremont Street, in the downtown area, was the original site of gaming in Las Vegas and had the first paved road in the area. The area expanded from this central street, eventually leading farther onto Las Vegas Boulevard. Today, Las Vegas is the largest city in Nevada and one of the fastest-growing in the nation.

Carson City, Lake Tahoe, and Reno
Nevada's capital, Carson City, is located in the sprawling Carson Valley. The historic downtown is unique in that small casinos line the same street as the capitol building. Over the mountains to the west, beautiful Lake Tahoe gleams from above in vivid blue. It's the largest alpine lake in the United States and straddles the border with California, with the Nevada side having multiple casino resorts. Reno, the Biggest Little City in the World, has a scenic Riverwalk District on the Truckee River downtown.

In the Wide-open Spaces
❑ Zephyr Cove, Lake Tahoe
❑ The Hoover Dam and Lake Mead National Recreation Area
❑ The Bighorn Sheep at Boulder City's Hemenway Park
❑ Laughlin, on the Colorado River
❑ Historic Genoa

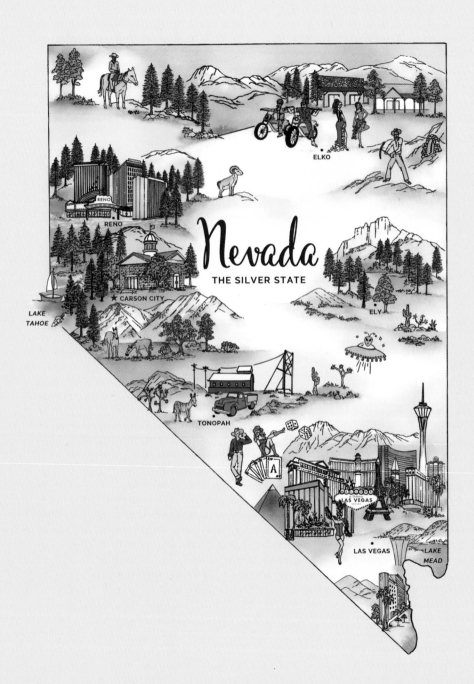

NEVADA

JUST THE FACTS

DATE(S) VISITED

TRAVEL COMPANION(S)

MODE OF TRANSPORTATION

WEATHER

LODGINGS

LOCAL Cuisine

Best state delicacy eaten _____

GETTING CULTURED

Museums or other points of interest visited

FIRST TIME?

Was this your first visit, or are you basically a local?

☐ YES ☐ NO

HAD TO SEE IT TO BELIEVE IT

Strangest tourist attraction visited _____

RATE THE STATE

☆ ☆ ☆ ☆ ☆

Oregon

— est. 1859 —

THE BEAVER STATE The Oregon Trail brought large numbers of settlers to Oregon territory in the mid-1800s. With plenty of beavers, fur trading became part of their livelihoods. Even traveling the waterways of Oregon today, maybe along the rushing Rogue River, you're likely to see a few busy beavers along the way—thus the state nickname.

STATE FACTS

State Capital: **Salem**
State Flower: **Oregon Grape**
State Bird: **Western Meadowlark**
Largest Forest: **Willamette National Forest**

Weird Days in Portland

Portland likes to keep things weird. In this city, you'll find a good share of offbeat shops and bookstores. It rains more than it shines and there are cozy coffeehouses to duck into on almost every corner. A classic Portland foodie haunt is Voodoo Doughnut, where their hot pink boxes of doughnuts are magically good. Strangeness rules the road here, with sites like Mill Ends Park, the "World's Smallest Park," a two-foot-wide city park in the middle of Naito Parkway. The outlying parks and gardens take you worlds away from urban life, including the lovely Portland Japanese Garden, a paradise of waterfalls, greenery, bridges, ponds, and areas designed for meditation. Whatever path you take in Portland will be an eclectic and memorable one!

Crater Lake National Park

Crater Lake is the deepest lake in the country and is six miles wide. Thousands of years ago, a large volcano erupted with such force that the mountain collapsed, inverting into the ground and creating a caldera. This crater filled with water over time to form the indigo lake that is enjoyed today.

The Oregon Coast

An excursion along the Oregon Coast takes you through one charming seaside village after another. When the fog rolls in, the beaches take on a misty allure, but when the sun breaks through, the striking scenery is unveiled. Summer months bring more crowds to Cannon Beach and Seaside, but along Oregon's 363 miles of coastline, there are plenty of secluded spots as well. The sea cliffs in Depoe Bay provide an elevated viewpoint for whale watching, although taking a charter cruise from the harbor brings you much closer to the action.

Wild Scenic Views

- ❏ Silver Falls State Park's Trail of Ten Falls
- ❏ Multnomah Falls in the Columbia River Gorge
- ❏ The Rogue River
- ❏ Bend Whitewater Park
- ❏ Natural Bridges Viewpoint on the coast
- ❏ Covered Bridges Scenic Bikeway in Eugene

ASTORIA •

COLUMBIA RIVER

• PORTLAND

PENDLETON •

SNAKE RIVER

SALEM

Oregon

THE

BEAVER STATE

PACIFIC
OCEAN

OREGON TRAIL

COOS BAY •

EUGENE •

CRATER LAKE

ROGUE RIVER

MEDFORD •

KLAMATH
FALLS •

• BROOKINGS

OREGON

JUST THE FACTS

DATE(S)
VISITED

TRAVEL
COMPANION(S)

MODE OF
TRANSPORTATION

WEATHER

LODGINGS

LOCAL Cuisine

Best state delicacy eaten _____

GETTING CULTURED

Museums or other points of interest visited

FIRST TIME?

Was this your first visit, or are you basically a local?

YES ☐   NO ☐

HAD TO SEE IT TO BELIEVE IT

Strangest tourist attraction visited _____

RATE THE STATE

☆ ☆ ☆ ☆ ☆

Utah

— est. 1896 —

THE BEEHIVE STATE Utah's state insect is the hard-working honeybee. The industrious people of Utah have been just as busy and dedicated as the bees for centuries, working together for the greater good of their communities. From the mountain peaks of Park City to the red buttes of Monument Valley, Utah is a place that calls to the wandering heart.

STATE FACTS

State Capital: **Salt Lake City**
State Flower: **Sego Lily**
State Bird: **California Seagull**
State Insect: **Honeybee**

Salt Lake City

Utah was settled by Mormon pioneers in 1847, after Brigham Young led them to the desolate Salt Lake Valley. The Salt Lake City Tabernacle reaches toward the sky in the center of downtown's Temple Square, its spires creating an iridescent glow against the skyline. The nearby Great Salt Lake is an anomaly within the dry desert. Minerals and salt drift into the lake from rivers, but there is no outlet, other than evaporation. This leaves the lake saltier than the ocean!

The Mighty Five

The Mighty Five national parks spanning southern Utah include Canyonlands, Arches, Bryce Canyon, Capitol Reef, and Zion. Moab is a good place to hang your hat for visits to Arches and Canyonlands. It's a mountain-bike utopia, with a bohemian downtown and several low-key lodging options. The most recognized arch in this territory is Delicate Arch, which you'll find on several souvenirs in Moab, but there's nothing quite like seeing it in person. Capitol Reef is centrally located and features Waterpocket Fold, a geological indentation in the Earth's surface. Moving farther west to Zion, the Virgin River flows in between looming red cliffs that cast their dark shadows upon the canyon's surface. Zion has intense hiking, including treading against the river's upstream flow through slot canyons in the Narrows or climbing a dangerously slim and steep trail to the summit of Angels Landing. Though close to Zion, Bryce Canyon's landscape of hoodoos sets it apart. (Hoodoos are rock formations of varying widths, heights, and textures, formed by a unique erosion process involving rain and ice.)

Epic Utah Experiences

- ❏ Antelope Island's free-roaming bison
- ❏ Monument Valley Navajo Tribal Park
- ❏ Brian Head
- ❏ Park City
- ❏ Horseshoe Bend in Glen Canyon National Recreation Area
- ❏ Springdale, near Zion National Park

THE GREAT
SALT LAKE

THE GREAT
SALT LAKE DESERT

KINGS PEAK

SALT LAKE
CITY

Utah

THE BEEHIVE STATE

MOAB

• ST. GEORGE • ZION

MONUMENT
VALLEY

UTAH

JUST THE FACTS

DATE(S) VISITED

TRAVEL COMPANION(S)

MODE OF TRANSPORTATION

WEATHER

LODGINGS

LOCAL *Cuisine*

Best state delicacy eaten _____

FIRST TIME?

Was this your first visit, or are you basically a local?

☐ YES ☐ NO

HAD TO SEE IT TO BELIEVE IT

Strangest tourist attraction visited _____

GETTING CULTURED

Museums or other points of interest visited

RATE THE STATE

☆☆☆☆☆

35

Washington

— est. 1889 —

THE EVERGREEN STATE Mount Rainier is an active volcano and the highest mountain peak in the lower forty-eight states. Standing almost 3 miles tall, its pinnacle is seen from great distances. The Cascade Range defines most of Washington's central landscape, but the mountainous ridges gradually become fruitful valleys, where fields of apples grow crisp and ripe. Along with apple orchards, Washington consistently ranks first in growing pears, cherries, and blueberries. Getting out in nature is easy in this state, simply because wherever you may be, scenic diversity and the fruits of life are all around you.

STATE FACTS

State Capital: **Olympia**
State Flower: **Coast Rhododendron**
State Bird: **American Goldfinch**
Highest Mountain: **Mount Rainier**

Waterfront Seattle

Seattle's skyline is marked by the iconic Space Needle, which debuted at the 1962 World's Fair during the "Age of Space." For decades since, Seattle has led with an innovative attitude; many technology companies are headquartered in the city. But Seattle also embraces the simple things in life. Since 1907, Pike Place Market has hosted farmers and crafters selling their goods. Among the rows of vegetable and fruit stands, fresh fish, ceramics, blown glass, and jewelry, the familiar aroma of fresh-brewed coffee pours out from the original Starbucks. On Pier 54 nearby, Ivar's Acres of Clams walk-up seafood bar serves some of the best clam and salmon chowders. Around the corner, the Ye Olde Curiosity Shop has sold strange novelties since 1899.

The Olympic Peninsula

The Olympic Peninsula lies between Hood Canal, the Strait of Juan de Fuca, and the Pacific Ocean. Olympic National Park bounds the evergreen forests within the middle of the peninsula, and there are also 73 miles of undeveloped coastline. Colossal rock formations go beyond the water's edge and Douglas fir, cedar, and spruce forests cradle the sea. Fog hangs low, shrouding the beaches in mystery. When the fog lifts, sometimes giant orcas and humpback whales pass by in the distance during their migrating seasons. Within rock crevices, an unbelievable assortment of sea urchins, anemones, starfish, and other creatures swirl into their hidden worlds in the tidepools of Kalaloch Beach. Because of the misty coastal air and frequent rains, the peninsula is home to four rainforests. The Hall of Mosses is a sensational hike in the Hoh Rainforest that immerses you in the greenery of enormous woodlands draped in moss.

Wanderlust in Washington

❏ Riverfront Spokane
❏ Flying kites in Long Beach
❏ Columbia River Gorge
❏ North Cascades National Park

PACIFIC
OCEAN

MT.
OLYMPUS

MT. VERNON

SEATTLE •

TACOMA

OLYMPIA

MT. RAINIER

Washington

THE EVERGREEN STATE

SPOKANE •

WALLA WALLA

VANCOUVER •

COLUMBIA RIVER

WASHINGTON

JUST THE FACTS

DATE(S)
VISITED

TRAVEL
COMPANION(S)

MODE OF
TRANSPORTATION

WEATHER

LODGINGS

LOCAL Cuisine

Best state delicacy eaten

GETTING CULTURED

Museums or other points of interest visited

FIRST TIME?

Was this
your
first visit,
or
are you
basically
a local?

YES ☐   NO ☐

HAD TO SEE IT TO BELIEVE IT

Strangest tourist
attraction visited

RATE THE STATE

☆☆☆☆☆

Wyoming

— est. 1890 —

THE EQUALITY STATE There has always been a pioneering spirit in Wyoming that has captivated our imaginations. It's a state that calls to the wild at heart, with its wide-open ranges. It was the first state to grant women the right to vote and also the first to elect a female governor. On the plains in the northeast corner of the state, a massive butte stands isolated on the horizon. This looming monolith, Devils Tower, became the first official national monument in the United States.

State Capital: **Cheyenne**
State Flower: **Indian Paintbrush**
State Bird: **Western Meadowlark**
Tallest Butte: **Devils Tower**

Yellowstone National Park

Although some of the 2.2 million acres cross into Idaho and Montana, most of Yellowstone lies within Wyoming. Formed by ancient volcanic activity, magma boils deep underground and is revealed in over 10,000 smoldering geothermal features. Walk directly around the rims of Morning Glory Pool and Grand Prismatic Spring, where steam ascends from colorful hot springs. Old Faithful, an active geyser that can spray water almost 200 feet in the air, erupts on its own schedule. You might also encounter bison, grizzly bears, or wolves in the open meadows. Yellowstone is raw to its core.

The Cowboy's Dream in Jackson Hole

An old wooden sign on the way to Jackson Hole reads, *Howdy Stranger, Yonder is Jackson Hole, the Last of the Old West.* Dude ranches began opening their doors to guests in the early 1900s, giving ordinary folks a chance to horseback ride and sit around a campfire. This began a valley tradition—when in Jackson Hole, anyone can live out their Western dream. In the town square at the city's center, you'll find the antler arches, a distinctive landmark, while fine art galleries, boutiques, steakhouses, and more extend outward for blocks. The Million Dollar Cowboy Bar's neon sign of a bucking bronco has been every cowboy's favorite watering hole since 1937. Seats at the bar are even saddles!

The "Oldest" Cabin

On the old Lincoln Highway, the owners of a gas station built a cabin to attract passing tourists. However, they didn't use standard building materials for Fossil Cabin, but rather 5,796 dinosaur bones found at nearby Como Bluff. Needless to say, the "Building that used to Walk," located halfway between Medicine Bow and Wilcox, became one of the oddest roadside attractions around.

Western Wandering in Wyoming

❑ Devils Tower National Monument
❑ Grand Teton National Park
❑ Downtown Cheyenne's Big Boots
❑ Buffalo Bill's town of Cody

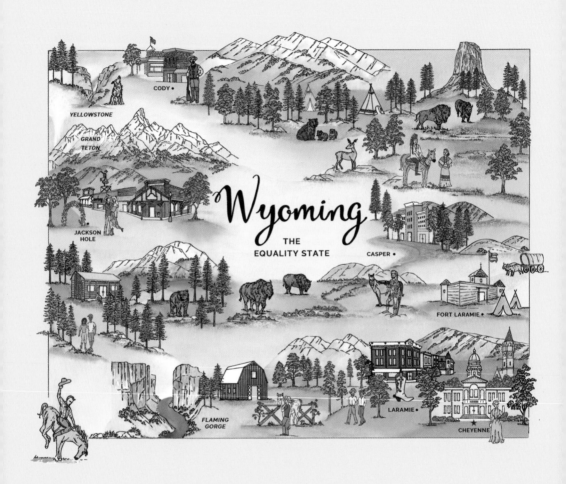

YELLOWSTONE

CODY •

GRAND
TETON

JACKSON
HOLE

Wyoming

THE
EQUALITY STATE

CASPER •

FORT LARAMIE •

FLAMING
GORGE

LARAMIE •

CHEYENNE

WYOMING

JUST THE FACTS

DATE(S) VISITED

TRAVEL COMPANION(S)

MODE OF TRANSPORTATION

WEATHER

LODGINGS

LOCAL Cuisine

Best state delicacy eaten _____

FIRST TIME?

Was this your first visit, or are you basically a local?

YES ☐   NO ☐

HAD TO SEE IT TO BELIEVE IT

Strangest tourist attraction visited _____

GETTING CULTURED

Museums or other points of interest visited

RATE THE STATE

☆ ☆ ☆ ☆ ☆

41

THE
SOUTHWEST

The Southwest has some of the most unique and varied scenery in the United States. Sweeping vistas of canyons and sandstone rock formations are abundant, but pine forests, prairies, and deserts also define the landscape. Native American and Hispanic heritage is prevalent, making for dynamic multicultural experiences. The diversity also extends to the wildlife, as many fascinating species live and thrive in the Southwest's rare climates. Enchanting and authentic destinations have inspired artists for centuries to capture the colorful vibrance of the region.

Arizona

— est. 1912 —

THE GRAND CANYON STATE Native American tribes, such as the Navajo and Hopi, have inhabited Arizona for thousands of years, living among the cliffs, deserts, and forests in pueblo dwellings. Wupatki, Canyon de Chelly, and Montezuma Castle are just a few of the many ancient relics within the state. Saguaro cacti, their soft, floral blossoms contrasting with their prickly skin, stand against a backdrop of buttes. The geography is diverse, ranging from thick forests to widespread deserts. Sunrise skies are a mix of turquoise, rust, and pink, and night skies are full of stars.

STATE FACTS

State Capital: **Phoenix**
State Flower: **Saguaro Cactus Blossom**
State Bird: **Cactus Wren**
State Reptile: **Ridge-nosed Rattlesnake**

Grand Canyon National Park

From the roots of the ponderosa pines growing firmly into its sides to the Bighorn sheep perched upon its steep cliffs, life has been cycling within the Grand Canyon's walls for millennia. The Colorado River appears only as a thin strand of blue from high above, winding along the canyon's floor. The most frequented area is the South Rim's Grand Canyon Village, where you'll find the historic El Tovar Hotel, Mary Colter's Lookout Studio, Hopi House, and more. It's also where the Grand Canyon Railway's steam locomotive has arrived at the depot from Williams since 1901.

Magical Sedona

The best way into Sedona is the Oak Creek Canyon Scenic Drive commencing in Flagstaff. This switchback road weaves through soaring red rock canyons covered in pines, eventually opening to the valley of Sedona below. Almost all the rock formations in the area hold native significance, and some serve as markers for Sedona's renowned vortexes. These vortexes are natural energy fields, not physically seen but often felt and believed to contain special powers. Keep an eye out for junipers twisted in whirlwind patterns as you get closer!

Lake Havasu's London Bridge

The original 1830s London Bridge was purchased in 1968 and shipped, brick by brick, from England to the US, before being rebuilt in the desert oasis of Lake Havasu on the Colorado River.

Arizona Road Trip Stops

❏ Wild West Junction in Williams on Route 66
❏ Standin' on the Corner Park in Winslow
❏ Downtown Flagstaff
❏ Saguaro National Park
❏ Old Town Scottsdale
❏ Legendary Tombstone
❏ Prescott's Whiskey Row

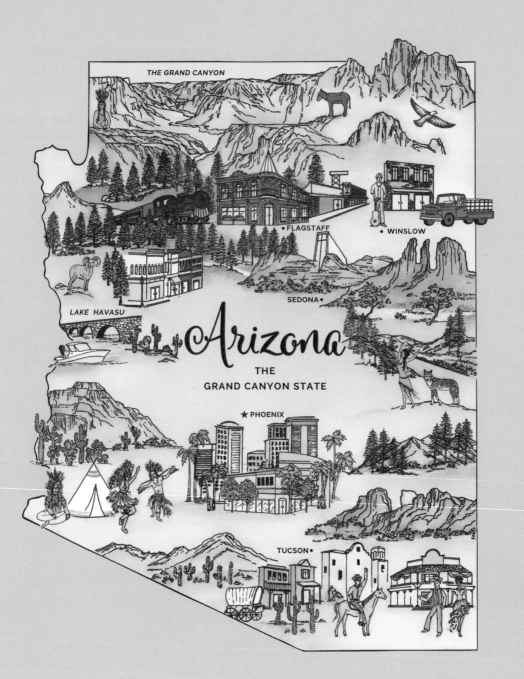

ARIZONA

JUST THE FACTS

DATE(S) VISITED

TRAVEL COMPANION(S)

MODE OF TRANSPORTATION

WEATHER

LODGINGS

LOCAL Cuisine

Best state delicacy eaten _____

GETTING CULTURED

Museums or other points of interest visited

FIRST TIME?

Was this your first visit, or are you basically a local?

☐ YES ☐ NO

HAD TO SEE IT TO BELIEVE IT

Strangest tourist attraction visited _____

RATE THE STATE

☆ ☆ ☆ ☆ ☆

New Mexico

— est. 1912 —

THE LAND OF ENCHANTMENT New Mexico draws visitors with its majestic natural beauty, cultural diversity, and artistic influence. The rich history of New Mexico originates with Native American tribes, who resided in pueblos throughout this area as early as 23,000 BC. In the mid-1500s, Spanish explorer Francisco Vázquez de Coronado found in the area a golden land, a "New" Mexico. The following four centuries would bring conflict and war, until the territory finally became the forty-seventh state in the Union. Today, the blending of Native American and Spanish cultures remains the very fabric of New Mexico's vibrant character and charm.

STATE FACTS

State Capital: **Santa Fe**
State Flower: **Yucca Flower**
State Bird: **Greater Roadrunner**
Popular Food: **Chile Pepper**

Santa Fe

New Mexico's state capital is known as "the City Different." Pueblo settlements in the area can be traced back as early as 900 AD, while Spanish colonization began in the early 1600s. The first trading post was built in 1603 and the Palace of the Governors was established in 1610 on the Plaza. Most of the original structures still stand today. In the early 1800s, the Old Santa Fe Trail, connecting Missouri to Santa Fe, was a popular trade route. American fur traders, Native Americans, and the Spanish once met to trade goods in the Plaza, a tradition continued today in modern shops, galleries, and restaurants. When Georgia O'Keeffe arrived in 1929, her art greatly contributed to the cultivation of Santa Fe's reputation as a mecca for the arts.

Get Your Kicks on Route 66

The most legendary road in America, Route 66, played a large part in bringing tourism to the state throughout the mid-twentieth century. As cars became more affordable, American wanderlust made this "Mother Road" a true pilgrimage. Tucumcari, Albuquerque, Gallup, and so many little towns along the way embrace the history of that time. Segments of the original road, along with nostalgic neon signs, motels, and restaurants, still exist. When traveling I-40, stop along the way to take a step back in time and experience what made America fall in love with the freedom of a good, old-fashioned road trip.

Enchanting Locations

- ❏ The Santa Fe Plaza
- ❏ Taos Pueblo
- ❏ El Santuario de Chimayo
- ❏ Roswell Aliens
- ❏ Silver City
- ❏ Albuquerque's KiMo Theatre
- ❏ The Rio Grande
- ❏ Carlsbad Caverns
- ❏ White Sands National Park

TAOS

SANTA FE

ALBUQUERQUE

GALLUP

New Mexico

THE
LAND OF ENCHANTMENT

ROSWELL •

SILVER CITY •

LAS CRUCES •

NEW MEXICO

JUST THE FACTS

DATE(S) VISITED

TRAVEL COMPANION(S)

MODE OF TRANSPORTATION

WEATHER

LODGINGS

LOCAL Cuisine

Best state delicacy eaten _____

_____

_____

_____

_____

_____

GETTING CULTURED

Museums or other points of interest visited

_____

_____

_____

_____

_____

FIRST TIME?

Was this your first visit, or are you basically a local?

☐ YES   ☐ NO

HAD TO SEE IT TO BELIEVE IT

Strangest tourist attraction visited _____

_____

_____

_____

_____

_____

RATE THE STATE

☆ ☆ ☆ ☆ ☆

Oklahoma

— est. 1907 —

THE SOONER STATE Oklahoma's nickname refers to "Sooners," settlers who claimed land in the state before it became available to purchase. Prior to their arrival, the territory was mainly inhabited by Native tribes, including the Caddo, Osage, Quapaw, and Wichita. In 1830, the Indian Removal Act granted the government authority to remove Indigenous peoples, such as the Choctaw, Creek, and Cherokee, from their homelands east of the Mississippi River and into present-day Oklahoma. The Trail of Tears refers to the long and brutal journey they made—a journey that thousands did not survive. Despite the darkness of that time, they pushed forward to build strong communities, and the spirit of their endurance lives on in Oklahoma.

STATE FACTS

State Capital: **Oklahoma City**
State Flower: **Oklahoma Rose**
State Bird: **Scissor-tailed Flycatcher**
Largest Protected Prairie: **Joseph H. Williams Tallgrass Prairie Preserve**

Old West History

In Oklahoma City, the National Cowboy & Western Heritage Museum is full of Western history. There are nearly 30,000 artifacts, including paintings, sculptures, and photographs of the frontier, as well as original paintings by Charles M. Russell, Frederic Remington, and Albert Bierstadt. Historical accounts of cattlemen, rodeos, and Native Americans reveal the complexity of how the West was forged. Upon entering, view James Earle Fraser's *End of the Trail* sculpture of a native man bent over his horse, having braved a battle through his exhaustion.

The Dust Bowl

During the 1930s, sections of Colorado, Kansas, New Mexico, Texas, and Oklahoma were devastated by severe dust storms, but the Oklahoma Panhandle suffered some of the worst damage. This catastrophe coincided with the Great Depression, giving farmers no choice but to leave their homes and head west to work in the fields of California. Documenting this was photographer Dorothea Lange, whose images of people residing in broken-down jalopies and shantytowns raised national awareness of their hardships. Folksinger Woody Guthrie's "This Land is Your Land" also came out of the dust. The Woody Guthrie Center in Tulsa features a rare collection of his belongings. To experience what living conditions were like in an authentic Dust Bowl house, visit the Cimarron Heritage Center in Boise City.

Enjoying the Great Outdoors
❏ Oklahoma City's Myriad Botanical Gardens
❏ Beavers Bend State Park
❏ Chickasaw National Recreation Area

BOISE CITY

Oklahoma

THE SOONER STATE

TULSA

ARKANSAS RIVER

OKLAHOMA CITY

LAWTON

RED RIVER

OKLAHOMA

JUST THE FACTS

DATE(S) VISITED

TRAVEL COMPANION(S)

MODE OF TRANSPORTATION

WEATHER

LODGINGS

LOCAL *Cuisine*

Best state delicacy eaten _____

GETTING CULTURED

Museums or other points of interest visited

FIRST TIME?

Was this your first visit, or are you basically a local?

☐ YES   ☐ NO

HAD TO SEE IT TO BELIEVE IT

Strangest tourist attraction visited _____

RATE THE STATE

☆☆☆☆☆

Texas

— est. 1845 —

THE LONE STAR STATE Prior to Texas becoming a state, it was its own country. After the Texas Revolution, the Texans succeeded in gaining independence from Mexico. The most legendary part of this war occurred at the Alamo in San Antonio, a historical fort where the Mexican army prevailed after a thirteen-day battle in 1836. "Remember the Alamo!" became the soldiers' mantra, serving as the motivation for their eventual victory in the war. The flag of Texas had only one star until it joined the Union, giving the state its nickname.

STATE FACTS

State Capital: **Austin**
State Flower: **Bluebonnet**
State Bird: **Mockingbird**
Popular Food: **Barbecue Brisket**

San Antonio

The Alamo was not just a military fort, but a Spanish mission. There are four other missions at San Antonio Missions National Historical Park. After spending time at this sacred site, make your way to the San Antonio River Walk, with pathways along the grand canal and bridges covered in moss. Enjoy plates of authentic Mexican cuisine at Casa Rio while seated outdoors under the shade of its multicolored umbrellas, then cruise the river on a boat tour.

Fort Worth

Long ago, the Fort Worth Stockyards were one of the last stops that cowboys made for supplies before crossing the Red River into uncharted territory. Years later, the railroad made it easier to ship cattle and the Union Stockyards was built as the new commerce center for livestock. The opening of the Cowtown Coliseum

followed, providing a venue for horse shows and rodeos that continue to this day. Stop into Billy Bob's Texas, "The World's Largest Honky Tonk," where country greats like Merle Haggard and Willie Nelson frequently played. Many musicians' cemented handprints hang on the wall.

Austin

Whether devouring smoked brisket at one of the barbecue joints or listening to live music, you'll find so much to do in this eclectic capital city. Austin's bat viewing is one of the oddities that "Keeps Austin Weird." From spring until fall, over one million Mexican free-tailed bats migrate to their beloved colony under the Congress Avenue Bridge. The best time to view the bats begins at dusk and continues into the night above Lady Bird Lake.

Big Tex Adventures

- ❑ Big Bend National Park on the Rio Grande
- ❑ Big Tex at the Texas State Fair
- ❑ Galveston's Pleasure Pier
- ❑ Gruene Hall, the oldest dance hall in Texas
- ❑ Houston's Hermann Park

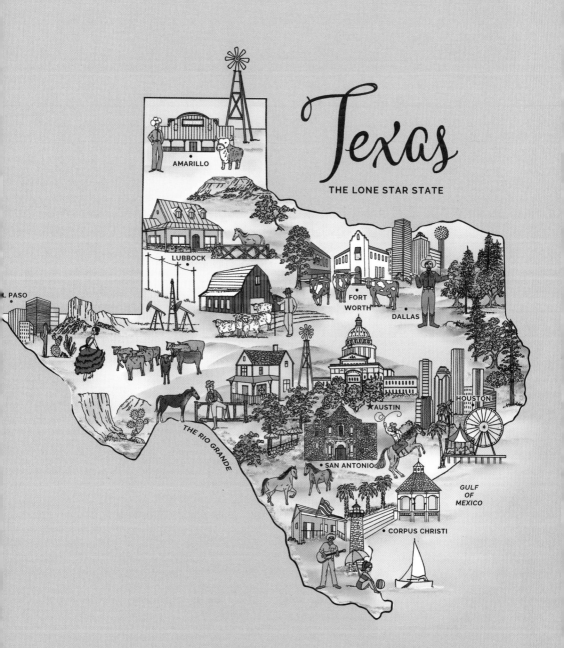

TEXAS

JUST THE FACTS

DATE(S) VISITED

TRAVEL COMPANION(S)

MODE OF TRANSPORTATION

WEATHER

LODGINGS

LOCAL Cuisine

Best state delicacy eaten _____

_____

_____

_____

_____

_____

GETTING CULTURED

Museums or other points of interest visited

_____

_____

_____

_____

_____

_____

FIRST TIME?

Was this your first visit, or are you basically a local?

YES ☐   NO ☐

HAD TO SEE IT TO BELIEVE IT

Strangest tourist attraction visited _____

_____

_____

_____

_____

_____

_____

RATE THE STATE

☆ ☆ ☆ ☆ ☆

THE
MIDWEST

The Midwest is America's heartland, where vast farmlands extend to the horizon, but large cities rise from the rolling hills and flat terrain. Though much of the Midwest is landlocked, countless lakes and rivers provide beautiful locations to fish, sail, and swim. When driving through the Midwestern states, take time to discover the natural beauty, charming small towns, and unusual roadside attractions the region has to offer.

Illinois

— est. 1818 —

THE PRAIRIE STATE Over half of Illinois was once sprawling, mixed-grass prairie. Little of the original landscape remains, as it now has plenty of trees and farmland instead. The Mississippi River forms the western boundary of the state, while the Ohio River defines the southern perimeter. Flowing in from Lake Michigan, the Chicago River intersects Chicago, creating its distinguished cityscape of skyscrapers soaring over the waterway (which also happens to run backward).

STATE FACTS

State Capital: **Springfield**
State Flower: **Violet**
State Bird: **Northern Cardinal**
Popular Food: **Chicago Hot Dog**

Chicago

Chicago is one of the most populated cities in America, and there is never a shortage of things to do. The Magnificent Mile is centered around North Michigan Avenue and is a lively shopping and dining hub. Also in this area, Millennium Park is home to Cloud Gate, a sculptural masterpiece nicknamed "The Bean." The stainless-steel sculpture reflects the skyline. Another one of Chicago's highlights is Navy Pier, which extends out into Lake Michigan. This pier has exhilarating rides and attractions, including the 200-foot-tall Centennial Wheel, which offers remarkable views of the city and lake. A visit to Chicago would not be complete without enjoying a Chicago-style hot dog, placed in a poppyseed bun and topped with sliced tomatoes, onions, and a pickle spear. There are several hot-dog

stands along the pier and parks surrounding the waterfront.

The Shawnee National Forest

Located between the Ohio and Mississippi Rivers, Shawnee National Forest covers 289,000 acres in southern Illinois. Stunning oak, hickory, and pine forests cradle rock formations protruding from the rolling hills. Its unique geographical location makes it a prime habitat for a variety of species. Garden of the Gods, one of the popular short hikes, provides panoramic views of the forest below.

Big Things in Small Town Casey

Casey is a small town that takes pride in its giant objects. It holds the official title for several Guinness World Records, such as the world's largest rocking chair, mailbox, gavel, barbershop pole, and teeter-totter, among others!

Favorite Roadside Detours

❏ The Leaning Tower of Niles
❏ The World's Largest Covered Wagon in Lincoln
❏ Chicago's Superdawg® Drive-In
❏ The Superman Statue in Metropolis

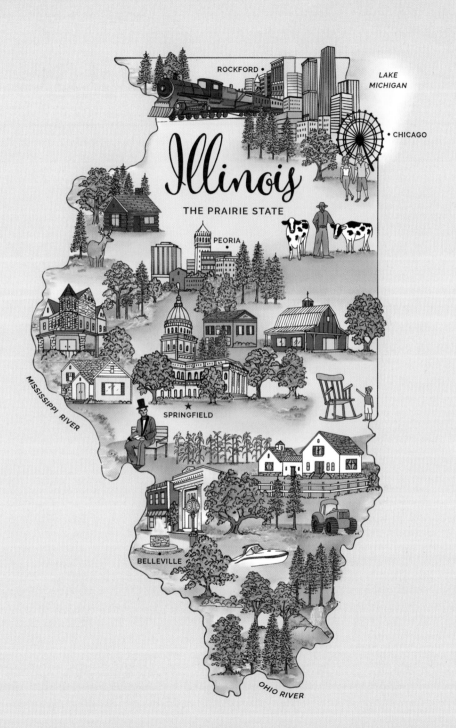

ROCKFORD •

LAKE MICHIGAN

• CHICAGO

Illinois

THE PRAIRIE STATE

PEORIA

MISSISSIPPI RIVER

SPRINGFIELD

BELLEVILLE

OHIO RIVER

ILLINOIS

JUST THE FACTS

DATE(S)
VISITED

TRAVEL
COMPANION(S)

MODE OF
TRANSPORTATION

WEATHER

LODGINGS

LOCAL Cuisine

Best state delicacy eaten _____

GETTING CULTURED

Museums or other points of interest visited

FIRST TIME?

Was this your first visit, or are you basically a local?

YES ☐ NO ☐

RATE THE STATE

HAD TO SEE IT TO BELIEVE IT

Strangest tourist attraction visited _____

Indiana

— est. 1816 —

THE HOOSIER STATE Located in the center of America's heartland, the spirit of Indiana is found in its reputation of friendly, humble, and welcoming Hoosiers. Though the origin of the word Hoosier is unknown, it's worn affectionately by those from Indiana. *Hoosiers*, the 1986 classic movie about a hometown basketball championship, depicts the state's pride in both the nickname and love for the game.

State Capital: **Indianapolis**
State Flower: **Peony**
State Bird: **Cardinal**
Popular Food: **Sugar Cream Pie**

Indianapolis

Indianapolis boasts the title Racing Capital of the World for its large number of motorsport races per year, including the greatest in auto racing, the Indy 500.

The Indianapolis Motor Speedway is acclaimed for being one of the oldest and largest speedways, with room to seat over 250,000 people. Even if you can't catch one of the races, the museum located at the speedway presents a staggering collection of race cars. Indianapolis also has a flourishing downtown that envelops Monument Circle, with the Soldiers' and Sailors' Monument at the center.

The Southern Indiana River Towns

In Southern Indiana, quaint and historical towns line the Ohio River across from Kentucky, and shipbuilding was the primary industry along this stretch of river. The towns of New Albany, Jeffersonville, and Madison sprang up from the Age of Steam. The prosperity of this time is evident in New Albany's Mansion Row Historic District, where affluent shipyard owners built their homes in the 1800s. Paddleboats still roll down the river as they have for over 200 years. Further northeast, Madison sits along the riverbank as a picture of Midwestern beauty. This charming town has one of the largest National Historic Landmark Districts in the United States, encompassing a total of 133 blocks.

Hoosier Adventures

❏ Carmel Arts & Design District
❏ Indiana Dunes National Park
❏ Wabash River Valley's Covered Bridges
❏ Antique Alley on Old National Road

INDIANA

JUST THE FACTS

DATE(S) VISITED

TRAVEL COMPANION(S)

MODE OF TRANSPORTATION

WEATHER

LODGINGS

LOCAL Cuisine

Best state delicacy eaten _____

_____

_____

_____

_____

_____

GETTING CULTURED

Museums or other points of interest visited

_____

_____

_____

_____

_____

FIRST TIME?

Was this your first visit, or are you basically a local?

☐ YES   ☐ NO

HAD TO SEE IT TO BELIEVE IT

Strangest tourist attraction visited _____

_____

_____

_____

_____

_____

RATE THE STATE

☆ ☆ ☆ ☆ ☆

Iowa

— est. 1846 —

THE HAWKEYE STATE Over half of Iowa is covered in corn and soybean fields and over a third of land is used for farming. Planting and harvesting have been a way of life on the plains of Iowa for centuries. When driving along the roadways, you'll find rural towns scattered in between nothing other than miles of fields. Few words sum it up better than the 1989 movie *Field of Dreams*: "Is this Heaven?" "No, it's Iowa." This line represents more than just baseball in a cornfield, but rather the vision of the American dream in its purest form.

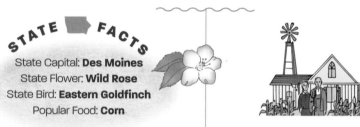

STATE FACTS

State Capital: **Des Moines**
State Flower: **Wild Rose**
State Bird: **Eastern Goldfinch**
Popular Food: **Corn**

The Iowa State Fair

Des Moines hosts the Iowa State Fair annually in August. With an average attendance of over one million people, it's the greatest celebration in Iowa! For eleven days, the fairgrounds take on an exciting pulse of whirling rides, petting zoos, agricultural displays, and corn dogs. Don't miss the world-famous Butter Cow, a 600-pound sculpture made of pure Iowa butter. Since 1911, when J.K. Daniels' butter cow first debuted, it's been a staple at the fair.

The Best Portrait Spot in Iowa

Grant Wood was an American artist from Iowa whose work revolved around the atmosphere of rural life. His iconic painting *American Gothic* depicts a rather stern man holding a pitchfork with a woman by his side in front of a farmhouse in Eldon, Iowa. This recognizable location is now a museum—and a nice backdrop for your next family portrait.

Famous Iowa Locations

- ❑ The *Field of Dreams* movie set in Dyersville
- ❑ Madison County's covered bridges
- ❑ Music Man Square in Mason City

MASON CITY •

Iowa

THE HAWKEYE STATE

CEDAR
RAPIDS •

★ DES MOINES •

MISSOURI RIVER

MISSISSIPPI RIVER

IOWA

JUST THE FACTS

DATE(S) VISITED

TRAVEL COMPANION(S)

MODE OF TRANSPORTATION

WEATHER

LODGINGS

LOCAL Cuisine

Best state delicacy eaten _____

GETTING CULTURED

Museums or other points of interest visited

FIRST TIME?

Was this your first visit, or are you basically a local?

☐ YES ☐ NO

HAD TO SEE IT TO BELIEVE IT

Strangest tourist attraction visited _____

RATE THE STATE

☆ ☆ ☆ ☆ ☆

Kansas

— est. 1861 —

THE SUNFLOWER STATE When driving the byways of Kansas, the sky somehow seems bigger and bluer against the flat horizon. From August through September, sunflowers come into their full bloom and cover the fields in yellow. This is the time of year when Kansas shows off its true splendor. When you think of Kansas, obviously *The Wizard of Oz* comes to mind, with Dorothy in her sparkly slippers and all the characters skipping down the yellow brick road. Kansas embraces its connection to the story with tourist spots like the OZ Museum in Wamego. A similar magic may be seen all over this whimsical state in small wonders blossoming under the rainbows.

STATE FACTS

State Capital: **Topeka**
State Flower: **Sunflower**
State Bird: **Western Meadowlark**
State Mammal: **American Buffalo**

Boot Hill in Dodge City

In the old Wild West, Dodge City was notorious for outlaws. In the "Wickedest Little City in the West," dance halls and saloons lined the dirt roads, where cowboys, gamblers, and wanderers off the Old Santa Fe Trail rode in for a good time. During Dodge City's heyday in the late 1800s, legends like Wyatt Earp and Doc Holliday lived in this dusty frontier. Put on your cowboy boots and spurs and step back in time at the Boot Hill Museum, located next to the Boot Hill Cemetery. In addition to artifacts, outlaws and sheriffs reenact gunslinging standoffs, and saloon girls kick up their heels to dance. During late summer, Dodge City Days takes over this rambling town with a rodeo and Longhorn cattle drives.

The Keeper of the Plains

At the confluence of the Little and Big Arkansas Rivers in Wichita, the Keeper of the Plains stands upon the rocks and reaches toward the sky. This sculpture honors the Native American Nations of the Great Plains. In recent years, smaller Keeper of the Plains sculptures painted by local artists have been placed around the city.

Along the Yellow Brick Road
- ❑ Botanica, the Wichita Gardens
- ❑ World's Largest Ball of Twine in Cawker City
- ❑ The Big Well in Greensburg
- ❑ The Yellow Brick Road in Sedan

65

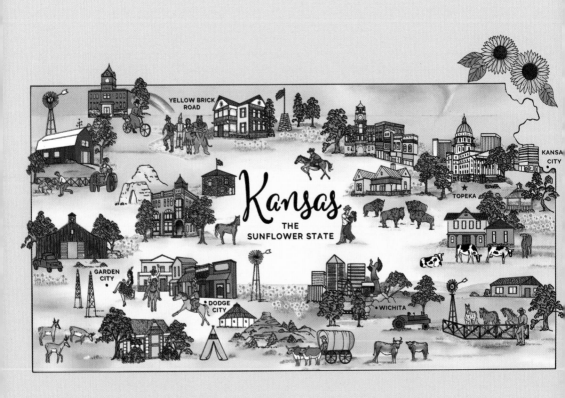

YELLOW BRICK
ROAD

KANSAS
CITY

Kansas

THE
SUNFLOWER STATE

TOPEKA

GARDEN
CITY

DODGE
CITY

WICHITA

KANSAS

JUST THE FACTS

DATE(S) VISITED

TRAVEL COMPANION(S)

MODE OF TRANSPORTATION

WEATHER

LODGINGS

LOCAL Cuisine

Best state delicacy eaten _____

GETTING CULTURED

Museums or other points of interest visited

FIRST TIME?

Was this your first visit, or are you basically a local?

YES ☐   NO ☐

RATE THE STATE

★ ★ ★ ★ ★

HAD TO SEE IT TO BELIEVE IT

Strangest tourist attraction visited _____

Michigan

— est. 1837 —

THE GREAT LAKES STATE Michigan is surrounded by four of the five Great Lakes. Driving along the shores, you'll spot a multitude of lighthouses—Michigan takes pride in being the state with the most lighthouses in the country! In addition to seeing the marvelous lakefronts and beautiful towns of its interior, take time to stop in the state's largest metropolis, Detroit, where Motown Records began and Henry Ford manufactured the first mass-produced automobile, the Model T.

STATE FACTS

State Capital: **Lansing**
State Flower: **Apple Blossom**
State Bird: **American Robin**
State Mammal: **White-tailed Deer**

Mackinac Island

Michigan is divided into two peninsulas. The connection of the upper and lower peninsulas is by way of the Mackinac Bridge, which extends over the strait where Lakes Michigan and Huron adjoin. The upper peninsula is more remote, with timbered woods spreading north to reach the pure waters of Lake Superior. Mackinac Island is slightly to the east of the upper peninsula, in Lake Huron. Almost frozen in a time, Mackinac Island is the jewel of the Great Lakes, where the elegance of the Grand Hotel meets the simple delicacy of homemade fudge. To get to the island, you must leave your car behind, as cars have been banned since the turn of the twentieth century. Most visitors park and take a short ferry ride from Mackinaw City or St. Ignace. Once you step foot on the island, you'll feel the old-fashioned ambiance. Horse-drawn carriages and bicycles are the common modes of transportation here, and Victorian buildings painted in pastel shades line Main Street.

See an Authentic Dutch Windmill in Holland!

The only authentic Dutch windmill in the United States is in Holland, Michigan. It was shipped from the Netherlands and reconstructed in 1964. In the spring, when the encompassing tulip garden comes into bloom, it's a lovely sight to admire.

Journeys in Michigan

- ❏ The Henry Ford Museum of American Innovation in Dearborn
- ❏ Eagle Harbor Lighthouse
- ❏ Frederik Meijer Gardens & Sculpture Park in Grand Rapids
- ❏ Tahquamenon Falls State Park

MICHIGAN

JUST THE FACTS

DATE(S) VISITED

TRAVEL COMPANION(S)

MODE OF TRANSPORTATION

WEATHER

LODGINGS

LOCAL Cuisine

Best state delicacy eaten _____

GETTING CULTURED

Museums or other points of interest visited

FIRST TIME?

Was this your first visit, or are you basically a local?

YES ☐   NO ☐

HAD TO SEE IT TO BELIEVE IT

Strangest tourist attraction visited _____

RATE THE STATE

☆ ☆ ☆ ☆ ☆

Minnesota

— est. 1858 —

THE NORTH STAR STATE In the Land of 10,000 Lakes, days spent on the sapphire waters of Lake Superior are far removed from the metropolis of the Twin Cities. Seasons change quickly, and warm nights under the stars turn to bundled-up evenings at ice hockey games. The North Star State received its nickname for having the northernmost point of any state in the lower forty-eight.

STATE FACTS

State Capital: **St. Paul**
State Flower: **Lady's Slipper**
State Bird: **Common Loon**
State Tree: **Red Pine**

The Twin Cities

The cities of Minneapolis and St. Paul form an extensive greater metropolitan area called the Twin Cities. The Mississippi River runs through the middle and meets the Minnesota River to the south. Amid the high-rises in central Minneapolis, the Mary Tyler Moore statue pays tribute to not only the show, but to working women everywhere. While visiting the area, Bloomington's Mall of America offers the greatest shopping experience of all time. You could shop for week and still not get to each store on all four levels of the mall, which also includes a full indoor amusement park.

A Mighty Drive on the Great River Road

The Great River Road begins at Itasca State Park in Park Rapids and follows the mighty Mississippi south to the Gulf of Mexico. Lake Itasca provides the Mississippi River with the water that flows 2,552 miles downstream from this point. A simple log with carved lettering marks the spot where the adventure begins. This scenic route will not only take you through ten states, but its enthralling landscapes will be etched into your memory for years to come.

Natural Surroundings

- ❏ The Boundary Waters
- ❏ The Minneapolis Sculpture Garden
- ❏ The National Eagle Center in Wabasha
- ❏ The North Shore of Lake Superior
- ❏ Paisley Park
- ❏ Split Rock Lighthouse State Park

Minnesota

THE NORTH STAR STATE

RED RIVER

LAKE SUPERIOR

• DULUTH

• ST. CLOUD

• MINNEAPOLIS

★ ST. PAUL

MINNESOTA RIVER

MISSISSIPPI RIVER

• WINONA

MINNESOTA

JUST THE FACTS

DATE(S) VISITED

TRAVEL COMPANION(S)

MODE OF TRANSPORTATION

WEATHER

LODGINGS

LOCAL Cuisine

Best state delicacy eaten _____

_____

_____

_____

_____

_____

GETTING CULTURED

Museums or other points of interest visited

_____

_____

_____

_____

_____

_____

_____

FIRST TIME?

Was this your first visit, or are you basically a local?

☐ YES ☐ NO

HAD TO SEE IT TO BELIEVE IT

Strangest tourist attraction visited _____

_____

_____

_____

_____

_____

_____

RATE THE STATE

☆ ☆ ☆ ☆ ☆

Missouri

— est. 1821 —

THE SHOW-ME STATE The roads and trails of America connect us—across towns and cities, cultures and legacies, and even time. At one point in the country's history, Missouri was the farthest western state, and beyond its border was the great unknown. During this period, westward expansion was at its height, marked by Americans pushing beyond borders on the shadowy promises of settling new frontiers. These trails west, for the most part, started in Missouri.

STATE FACTS

State Capital: **Jefferson City**
State Flower: **White Hawthorn**
State Bird: **Eastern Bluebird**
State Tree: **Flowering Dogwood**

The Lake of the Ozarks
Nestled in the Ozark Mountains, the Lake of the Ozarks is a man-made reservoir and one of America's best vacation spots. The lake curves like a dragon, forming coves. Osage Beach is considered the heart of the lake for its number of resorts, dining options, and nightlife. However, with an astounding 1,150 miles of shoreline, there are many areas to discover around this lakeside retreat.

Gateway Arch National Park
The Gateway Arch in St. Louis is one of the greatest engineering marvels in the world. At 630 feet tall and 630 feet wide, the stainless-steel arch, designed by Eero Saarinen, remains the tallest ever built. The tram to the top takes you inside the structure to the observation deck overlooking the city and the Mississippi River below. This monument was intended to symbolize the pioneers who passed through St. Louis, their "gateway" to the west.

Did you know? Sumner, Missouri, is the "Wild Goose Capital of the World." The giant sculpture of Maxie the migrating goose on Route 139 pays tribute to the town's flocks.

Show Me Some More
- [ ] Country Club Plaza in Kansas City
- [ ] Downtown Springfield
- [ ] Joplin on Route 66
- [ ] Independence Square
- [ ] Meramec Caverns

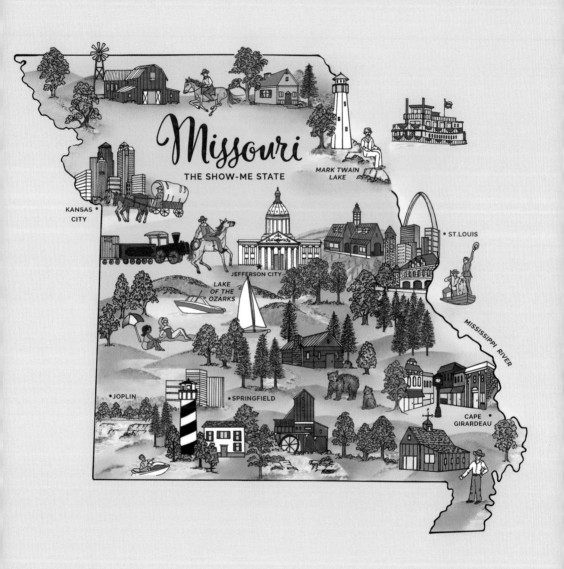

Missouri

THE SHOW-ME STATE

MARK TWAIN LAKE

KANSAS CITY

ST.LOUIS

MISSISSIPPI RIVER

JEFFERSON CITY

LAKE OF THE OZARKS

JOPLIN

SPRINGFIELD

CAPE GIRARDEAU

MISSOURI

JUST THE FACTS

DATE(S) VISITED

TRAVEL COMPANION(S)

MODE OF TRANSPORTATION

WEATHER

LODGINGS

LOCAL Cuisine

Best state delicacy eaten _____

GETTING CULTURED

Museums or other points of interest visited

FIRST TIME?

Was this your first visit, or are you basically a local?

☐ YES ☐ NO

HAD TO SEE IT TO BELIEVE IT

Strangest tourist attraction visited _____

RATE THE STATE

☆ ☆ ☆ ☆ ☆

Nebraska

— est. 1867 —

THE CORNHUSKER STATE Nebraska's landscape is defined by the Great Plains, and it was nicknamed the Cornhusker State for its substantial corn production. Prior to statehood, Native American tribes such as the Otoe-Missouria, Omaha, and Pawnee occupied the territory for centuries. However, with the age of western expansion came pioneers crossing the land on the Oregon, California, and Mormon Trails. Chimney Rock National Historic Site was a prime landmark for their journey west, but the nearby area encompassing Scotts Bluff National Monument was once home to multiple Native nations and their arrival ultimately altered the indigenous way of life. These national sites and monuments continue to be held sacred by the Native communities in Nebraska.

STATE FACTS

State Capital: **Lincoln**
State Flower: **Goldenrod**
State Bird: **Western Meadowlark**
Largest Lake: **Lake McConaughy**

Omaha

Omaha is renowned for its fine steakhouses, which have made the city the Steak Capital of the World. Whether you're having a filet, chicken-fried steak, or a Rueben, it's all about the meat in this city. After enjoying a good ol' Omaha meal, walk downtown to the corner of 16th and Dodge, where you'll find a collection of striking statues depicting bygone scenes from Nebraska's pioneer days at First National's Spirit of Nebraska's Wilderness and Pioneer Courage Park.

A True Roadside Attraction

In a remote field north of Alliance on Highway 87, Nebraska's oddest roadside detour has stood upright as a quirky marvel since 1987. Jim Reinders and his family constructed Carhenge, their own version of England's Stonehenge, using—you guessed it—old cars painted gray. Much like the ancient stones, the formation's circular arrangement casts shadows that follow the natural course of the sun's patterns.

Onward You Go!

- ❏ The Great Platte River Road Archway Monument in Kearney
- ❏ Downtown Lincoln
- ❏ North Platte's Buffalo Bill Ranch State Historical Park Museum
- ❏ Smith Falls State Park
- ❏ Sunken Gardens in Lincoln

NEBRASKA

JUST THE FACTS

DATE(S) VISITED

TRAVEL COMPANION(S)

MODE OF TRANSPORTATION

WEATHER

LODGINGS

LOCAL Cuisine

Best state delicacy eaten _____

GETTING CULTURED

Museums or other points of interest visited

FIRST TIME?

Was this your first visit, or are you basically a local?

☐ YES ☐ NO

HAD TO SEE IT TO BELIEVE IT

Strangest tourist attraction visited _____

RATE THE STATE

☆ ☆ ☆ ☆ ☆

North Dakota

— est. 1821 —

THE PEACE GARDEN STATE North Dakota is famous for enormous roadside attractions set against the grasslands. Awaiting you here are quirky statues such as the World's Largest Cow Sculpture, a supersized Holstein cow named Salem Sue in New Salem, and the World's Largest Buffalo, a gigantic bison in Jamestown's Frontier Village. Beyond the larger-than-life sculptures, natural wonders make North Dakota an incredible state. From the exquisite International Peace Garden that straddles the Canadian border, to the badlands of Theodore Roosevelt National Park, the diverse environments are nothing short of captivating.

STATE FACTS

State Capital: **Bismarck**
State Flower: **Wild Prairie Rose**
State Bird: **Western Meadowlark**
Popular Food: **Honey**

Did you know? North Dakota produces more honey than any other state!

The Badlands

The badlands of North Dakota are on the western side of the state. Canyons and buttes stretch as far as the eye can see. President Theodore Roosevelt proclaimed this area "where the romance of my life began." Theodore Roosevelt National Park contains some of the most scenic badlands in America. Bison roam and wild horses gallop against dramatic skies.

The Enchanted Highway

Grab your camera for this route! The Enchanted Highway begins at exit 72 off I-94 and ends in Regent, and it features giant roadside sculptures such as *Pheasants on the Prairie*, the World's Largest Tin Family, and *Geese in Flight*, just to name a few.

The Red River Market

If you find yourself in Fargo, make sure to schedule a stop at the Red River Market. Every Saturday in the summer and fall, local farmers and food vendors gather to share their wares with thousands of North Dakotans and visitors alike. The Red River Market emphasizes community, creating a space for all people to sample locally grown foods and for talented musicians and cultural performers to have their time in the sun!

Roadside Attractions

- ❏ Minot's Scandinavian Heritage Park
- ❏ The W'eel Turtle in Dunseith
- ❏ *Teddy Roosevelt Rides Again* in Regent
- ❏ Frontier Village in Jamestown

North Dakota

THE
PEACE GARDEN STATE

MINOT

GRAND FORKS

THE BADLANDS

BISMARCK

JAMESTOWN

FARGO

NORTH DAKOTA

JUST THE FACTS

DATE(S) VISITED

TRAVEL COMPANION(S)

MODE OF TRANSPORTATION

WEATHER

LODGINGS

LOCAL Cuisine

Best state delicacy eaten _____

FIRST TIME?

Was this your first visit, or are you basically a local?

YES ☐ NO ☐

GETTING CULTURED

Museums or other points of interest visited

HAD TO SEE IT TO BELIEVE IT

Strangest tourist attraction visited _____

RATE THE STATE

☆☆☆☆☆

Ohio

— est. 1803 —

THE BUCKEYE STATE Ohio's major cities of Cleveland, Columbus, Cincinnati, and Toledo overflow with interesting things to see. Beyond the urban areas, much of the state is covered in farms. While Ohio's terrain is generally flat, the southeastern corner is an exception. Resting at the foothills of the Appalachian Mountains, Ohio's Hill Country is lush with ample hills, rocky formations, waterfalls, and forests.

STATE FACTS

State Capital: **Columbus**
State Flower: **Red Carnation**
State Bird: **Cardinal**
State Tree: **Ohio Buckeye**

Rockin' It in Cleveland

On the edge of Lake Erie, Cleveland is home to the Rock & Roll Hall of Fame. The outside of the museum features an eye-catching glass pyramid, but the inside is even more gripping. Hundreds of guitars and other rock artifacts are displayed, including Jim Morrison's sherpa jacket, Ringo's drums, and Michael Jackson's rhinestone glove. This ultimate music-lover experience showcases the legacy of the world's greatest rock performers and their contributions to music.

The American Sign Museum

Inside an offbeat brick building in Cincinnati, discover an expansive museum completely dedicated to American signage. Vintage, hand-painted signs from as early as the 1800s

hang alongside their glowing neon counterparts. After spending time at the museum, don't forget to try a steaming bowl of Cincinnati chili at one of the several famed chili "parlors" throughout the city.

Little Switzerland

Sugarcreek is referred to as Ohio's Little Switzerland. In the village center, the World's Largest Cuckoo Clock keeps the time, with wooden dancers spinning to polka music every thirty minutes.

Unique Destinations in Ohio

- ❑ The Antique Stores in Springfield
- ❑ The Columbus Zoo and Aquarium
- ❑ Cedar Point Amusement Park in Sandusky
- ❑ The Pro Football Hall of Fame in Canton
- ❑ Cincinnati's Findlay Market
- ❑ The Ohio River Trail

Ohio

THE BUCKEYE STATE

TOLEDO

CLEVELAND

LAKE ERIE

GRAND LAKE

COLUMBUS ★

CINCINNATI

OHIO RIVER

OHIO

JUST THE FACTS

DATE(S)
VISITED

TRAVEL
COMPANION(S)

MODE OF
TRANSPORTATION

WEATHER

LODGINGS

LOCAL Cuisine

Best state delicacy eaten _____

FIRST TIME?

Was this your first visit, or are you basically a local?

☐ YES   ☐ NO

HAD TO SEE IT TO BELIEVE IT

Strangest tourist attraction visited _____

GETTING CULTURED

Museums or other points of interest visited

RATE THE STATE

☆☆☆☆☆

South Dakota

— est. 1889 —

THE MOUNT RUSHMORE STATE South Dakota has both the dense forests of the Black Hills and starkly barren badlands. In the Black Hills near Keystone, Mount Rushmore took fourteen years of strenuous construction before its 1941 completion. Nearby, construction of the Crazy Horse Memorial began in 1948, but has yet to be completed. When completed, it will be the largest sculpture in the world.

STATE FACTS

State Capital: **Pierre**
State Flower: **Pasque**
State Bird: **Ring-necked Pheasant**
State Tree: **Black Hills Spruce**

The Black Hills

The Black Hills is a sacred place to the Lakota, Dakota, and other Native nations. The name stems from the appearance of darkness it has from a distance, due to the heavy concentration of pines. When gold was discovered in 1874, Deadwood was born overnight and emerged as a wild boomtown. Hundreds flocked to the Black Hills, causing a wave of development. Deadwood continues to stay true to its Wild West persona today, with a good amount of casinos and saloons downtown. Farther to the south, bison and wild donkeys still walk the plains of Custer State Park. Among the many sights to behold in this precious national forest, Mount Rushmore should be your first stop.

Prehistoric South Dakota

The Jurassic history of this area may not be the first thing to come to mind, but South Dakota takes a lot of pride in its prehistoric ancestors. Numerous dinosaur sculptures on the side of road and at tourist spots highlight this history. Rapid City's Dinosaur Park is a fun place to take photos with oversized cement dinosaurs. Throughout the state, you'll also come across many museums housing authentic fossils dating back millions of years.

You Can't Miss Wall Drug

On the way to Badlands National Park, signs off the highway lead to the famed Wall Drug. Opened in 1931, Wall Drug began advertising free water and cups of coffee for a nickel to travelers passing through town. While this simple tradition continues, it's expanded into one of America's largest drug stores, complete with a restaurant, multiple souvenir shops, and other fun attractions. Make sure to try the warm homemade doughnuts!

Roaming Through South Dakota

❑ Biker Culture in Sturgis
❑ Mitchell's Corn Palace
❑ Sioux Falls Waterfalls
❑ Spearfish
❑ Reptile Gardens in Rapid City

SOUTH DAKOTA

JUST THE FACTS

DATE(S)
VISITED

TRAVEL
COMPANION(S)

MODE OF
TRANSPORTATION

WEATHER

LODGINGS

LOCAL Cuisine

Best state delicacy eaten _____

_____
_____
_____
_____
_____

FIRST TIME?

Was this your first visit, or are you basically a local?

☐ YES ☐ NO

HAD TO SEE IT TO BELIEVE IT

Strangest tourist attraction visited _____

_____
_____
_____
_____
_____

GETTING CULTURED

Museums or other points of interest visited

_____
_____
_____
_____
_____

RATE THE STATE

☆ ☆ ☆ ☆ ☆

Wisconsin

— est. 1848 —

THE BADGER STATE Wisconsin winters are bitterly cold, but when the snow melts in spring, the state transforms into a playground for water sports and adventures under the sun. There are over 15,000 lakes within the state, not to mention Lake Michigan along the western coast, and the entire northern perimeter borders on Lake Superior. Wisconsin is also known for cheese, beer, football, and Harleys. The dynamic city of Milwaukee is nicknamed "Brew City" for its number of breweries, and it's also where Harley-Davidson originated.

STATE FACTS

State Capital: **Madison**
State Flower: **Wood Violet**
State Bird: **American Robin**
Popular Food: **Fried Cheese Curds**

The Wisconsin Dells

The Dells is a segment of the Wisconsin River that bends for five miles through sandstone rock cliffs. Rock formations arise from the water and create mazes along the river. Because of this, the landscape and twists of the gorge are best viewed by taking one of the pontoon boat tours. Hiking the Dells gives a different outlook on the bizarre terrain, with one of the strangest hikes being the Witches Gulch trail, leading through slot canyons on wooden planks. Along with its magnificent scenery, the Dells is "The Waterpark Capital," boasting over twenty waterparks!

The Cheesy Side of Wisconsin

Wisconsin is "America's Dairyland," with thousands of dairy farms throughout the state. A love of cheese spreads into the culture as much as the cuisine. Locals proudly refer to themselves as "cheeseheads," sporting large cheese block hats at Green Bay Packers games. Even the welcome sign of the small town of Plymouth reads, "Cheese Capital of the World." Perhaps out of all the different flavors and ways to prepare cheese, Wisconsinite's love their cheese curds best. Ellsworth proclaims to be "The Cheese Curd Capital" and celebrates its notoriety with an annual Cheese Curd Festival. Whatever part of Wisconsin you visit, make sure to try the variety of cheeses!

Stunning Scenic Locations
❑ The Apostle Islands
❑ The St. Croix Valley
❑ Lake Geneva
❑ Green Bay Botanical Garden

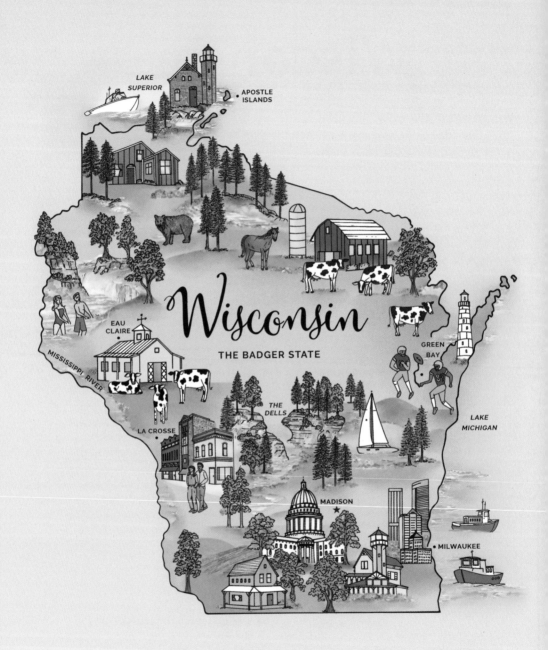

LAKE SUPERIOR

APOSTLE ISLANDS

Wisconsin

THE BADGER STATE

MISSISSIPPI RIVER

EAU CLAIRE

LA CROSSE

THE DELLS

GREEN BAY

LAKE MICHIGAN

MADISON

MILWAUKEE

WISCONSIN

JUST THE FACTS

DATE(S)
VISITED

TRAVEL
COMPANION(S)

MODE OF
TRANSPORTATION

WEATHER

LODGINGS

LOCAL Cuisine

Best state delicacy eaten _____

_____
_____
_____
_____
_____

GETTING CULTURED

Museums or other points of interest visited

_____
_____
_____
_____
_____
_____
_____
_____

FIRST TIME?

Was this your first visit, or are you basically a local?

☐ YES ☐ NO

RATE THE STATE

☆ ☆ ☆ ☆ ☆

HAD TO SEE IT TO BELIEVE IT

Strangest tourist attraction visited _____

_____
_____
_____
_____
_____
_____
_____

NEW ENGLAND

~~~

Quaint seaside villages, cozy mountain towns, and a few bustling cities give New England its distinct character. Fresh air, ocean views, and delicious seafood set the coast apart as one of the most idyllic places to unwind on a scenic road trip. Each season brings its own form of beauty, though the early fall is particularly special, when the leaves change to vibrantly warm colors. Along with its natural wonders, there are many ways to explore New England's rich history of early settlement and colonization throughout the region.

Connecticut

— est. 1788 —

THE CONSTITUTION STATE Connecticut is hailed as the Constitution State, because even though the Constitution was written in Pennsylvania, an agreement called the Fundamental Orders was written in Connecticut. Historians widely believe this agreement was a preliminary model for the Constitution. Connecticut is also considered the "Nutmeg State," though the origins of this spicy nickname are unknown. Nevertheless, locals love the flavor of nutmeg—it's an ingredient found in many Connecticut dishes.

STATE FACTS

State Capital: **Hartford**
State Flower: **Mountain Laurel**
State Bird: **American Robin**
Popular Food: **Apple Cider Doughnuts**

Maritime History

Connecticut's maritime history reaches back to the 1600s. Seaside villages such as Mystic and New London were integral to shipbuilding. From the 1700s to the early 1900s, Mystic was a bustling harbor community. Today, the famed Mystic Seaport Museum and Seaport Village offer a glimpse into its nautical heritage. Head back up to Groton, just across the river from New London, to spend the day aboard the USS *Nautilus*, a decommissioned submarine-turned-museum!

The Litchfield Hills Region

Tucked in the northwest corner of Connecticut is an area characterized by small lakes, rolling hills, and twenty-one charming New England towns. It's the perfect place to spend an afternoon fishing, rowing, or paddleboarding. Summertime is beautiful in the Litchfield Hills, but it's also recognized for having gorgeous foliage and rural pumpkin patches in the fall.

New England Charm to Explore

- ❏ Gillette Castle State Park
- ❏ The Mark Twain House & Museum in Hartford
- ❏ Rocky Neck State Park
- ❏ The Barnum Museum in Bridgeport
- ❏ Weir Farm National Historical Park

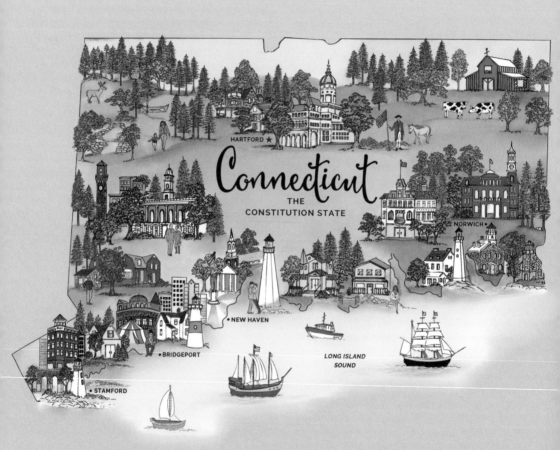

CONNECTICUT

JUST THE FACTS

DATE(S)
VISITED

TRAVEL
COMPANION(S)

MODE OF
TRANSPORTATION

WEATHER

LODGINGS

LOCAL Cuisine

Best state delicacy eaten _____

_____

_____

_____

_____

_____

FIRST TIME?

Was this your first visit, or are you basically a local?

YES ☐   NO ☐

HAD TO SEE IT TO BELIEVE IT

Strangest tourist attraction visited _____

_____

_____

_____

_____

_____

_____

GETTING CULTURED

Museums or other points of interest visited

_____

_____

_____

_____

_____

RATE THE STATE

☆ ☆ ☆ ☆ ☆

Maine

— est. 1820 —

THE PINE TREE STATE With peaceful seaside towns and pine forests that meet the ocean, Maine is a postcard of beauty. Along the coast, the fog layer provides a blanket of coolness to the air. On the water, fishing boats are seen through the mist and foghorns are heard in the distance. Lobster is served everywhere, and seafood shacks offer the morning's fresh catch. One can get lost in the tranquility of nature in Maine's untouched landscapes. Some of the 4,000 outlying islands are only accessible by boat. Midsize cities like Portland and Augusta are hubs for arts, culture, and flavorful culinary scenes. The state's motto, *Dirigo*, means "I lead" in Latin.

STATE FACTS

State Capital: **Augusta**
State Flower: **White Pine Cone**
State Bird: **Black-capped Chickadee**
Popular Food: **Lobster Rolls**

Acadia National Park's Special Sunrise

Acadia, located on Mount Desert Island, is the only national park in New England. This land is sacred to the native Wabanaki people, who have lived in Maine for thousands of years. Their name means "People of the Dawnland," and it derives from their connection to Acadia's Cadillac Mountain. From October to May, this mountain is typically where the first morning's light may be seen in the United States, peeking over the ocean's horizon. When visiting Acadia, Bar Harbor is a convenient place to stay on the island and is closest to the park entrance.

In the Heart of Bangor

Stephen King was born in Portland and has lived in Bangor for most of his life. In an otherwise normal neighborhood, his Victorian home is easily recognized for its vibrant red exterior and black, wrought-iron gate adorned with bats. Several of his stories, such as *It*, are set in fictional small towns in Maine.

Locations to See on the Coast

- ❑ Kennebunkport's Dock Square
- ❑ Maine's oldest lighthouse, Portland Head Light
- ❑ Camden on Penobscot Bay
- ❑ Bar Harbor
- ❑ Old Orchard Beach

Maine

THE
PINE TREE STATE

BANGOR

★ AUGUSTA

• LEWISTON

• PORTLAND

GULF
OF
MAINE

ATLANTIC
OCEAN

MAINE

JUST THE FACTS

DATE(S) VISITED

TRAVEL COMPANION(S)

MODE OF TRANSPORTATION

WEATHER

LODGINGS

LOCAL Cuisine

Best state delicacy eaten _____

_____

_____

_____

_____

GETTING CULTURED

Museums or other points of interest visited

_____

_____

_____

_____

_____

_____

FIRST TIME?

Was this your first visit, or are you basically a local?

☐ YES   ☐ NO

HAD TO SEE IT TO BELIEVE IT

Strangest tourist attraction visited _____

_____

_____

_____

_____

_____

_____

RATE THE STATE

☆ ☆ ☆ ☆ ☆

Massachusetts

— est. 1788 —

1620

THE BAY STATE Just over four centuries ago, one hundred passengers took a long journey across the Atlantic from the United Kingdom on the *Mayflower*. Seeking a new way of life, these early pioneers came to be known as the Pilgrims. The arrival of the Pilgrims marked the beginning of a European migration to the Americas. Massachusetts is an incredible state to visit for those who like history.

State Capital: **Boston**
State Flower: **Mayflower**
State Bird: **Black-capped Chickadee**
Popular Food: **New England Clam Chowder**

The Witches of Salem

Salem's connection to witchcraft has made it one of the most haunted towns in America. In 1692, the Salem witch trials began; by the end, over 200 souls were accused of practicing witchcraft, and several were hanged. The gothic architecture of the Salem Witch Museum is particularly spooky, but the collection is full of fascinating history, delving into the superstitions as well as the tainted history of that period.

Boston

Boston is one of the oldest cities in the United States. Founded in 1630, it became the center of colonial politics and a major seaport. The Massachusetts State House overlooks Beacon Hill, a neighborhood with historic row houses and gaslit streetlights. Many of America's firsts happened here, including the founding of the first college, Harvard, built in 1636,

and the creation of the first major league ballpark, Fenway Park, built in 1912. The combined energies of history, innovation, and education make Boston a well-rounded city.

The Cape

Extending into the Atlantic Ocean, Cape Cod's hook shape forms Cape Cod Bay. Miles of gorgeous beaches and charming seaside villages have long been beloved retreats for summer vacations. Just south of Cape Cod, the beautiful islands of Martha's Vineyard and Nantucket may be reached by ferry.

Did you know? **Within the area of Lexington and Concord, the "shot heard round the world" was fired to ignite the Revolutionary War. Minuteman statues in both towns pay tribute to the soldiers. Minute Man National Historical Park in Lincoln is the site of many of the war's opening battles.**

"Wicked-Fun" Things to Do

☐ Boston's Quincy Market
☐ The Amazing World of Dr. Seuss Museum in Springfield
☐ Whydah Pirate Museum in West Yarmouth

Massachusetts

THE BAY STATE

WORCESTER •

• SPRINGFIELD

• SALEM

★ BOSTON

ATLANTIC
OCEAN

CAPE
COD

• PLYMOUTH

NANTUCKET
SOUND

MARTHA'S
VINEYARD

NANTUCKET
ISLAND

MASSACHUSETTS

JUST THE FACTS

DATE(S)
VISITED

TRAVEL
COMPANION(S)

MODE OF
TRANSPORTATION

WEATHER

LODGINGS

LOCAL Cuisine

Best state delicacy eaten _____

_____

_____

_____

_____

_____

FIRST TIME?

Was this your first visit, or are you basically a local?

YES ☐ NO ☐

HAD TO SEE IT TO BELIEVE IT

Strangest tourist attraction visited _____

_____

_____

_____

_____

_____

_____

GETTING CULTURED

Museums or other points of interest visited

_____

_____

_____

_____

_____

RATE THE STATE

☆ ☆ ☆ ☆ ☆

New Hampshire

— est. 1788 —

THE GRANITE STATE New Hampshire is in the heart of New England. It's a state where summer days at the lake go on until sundown and apple pie, with a touch of maple, is served at the local diner. There is a feeling of comfort in the mountain air and small towns. As summer turns to fall, the leaves become brilliant shades of red, orange, and yellow, covering the hillsides with an autumn glow.

STATE FACTS

State Capital: **Concord**
State Flower: **Purple Lilac**
State Bird: **Purple Finch**
Tallest Mountain: **Mount Washington**

The Mount Washington Cog Railway

Mount Washington, in the White Mountains, is the highest peak in the northeastern region of the United States. For an adventure of a lifetime, take the oldest steam locomotive—the Cog Railway—to the summit. Riding this train has been a thrill since 1869, giving those brave enough to handle the steep incline the reward of an incredible vista once at the top. Mount Washington is also recognized for having dramatic weather phenomena and wind speeds have reached a shocking 231 miles per hour!

Downtown Manchester

The Merrimack River flows through the center of Manchester, and one of the best ways to enjoy the river's scenery is by walking the Heritage Trail. Along this route, you'll notice colorful shapes painted on the riverfront steps as the trail leads through Arms Park, patterns alluding to the city's textile legacy and the nearby historic Millyard District. While in the area, make sure to grab a bite at the Red Arrow Diner. Open since 1922, it's one of the smallest, yet most famous, diners in the country! Don't be surprised to see a familiar face, as many celebrities and politicians have been known to stop by.

Memorable Destinations

- ❏ Portsmouth's Market Square
- ❏ Clark's Bears in Lincoln
- ❏ Flume Gorge in Franconia Notch State Park
- ❏ The Black Heritage Trail of New Hampshire in Portsmouth
- ❏ Lake Winnipesaukee
- ❏ Sculptured Rocks Natural Area

MT. WASHINGTON

New
Hampshire

THE GRANITE STATE

CONCORD

DOVER •

• PORTSMOUTH

MANCHESTER •

ATLANTIC
OCEAN

NEW HAMPSHIRE

JUST THE FACTS

DATE(S) VISITED

TRAVEL COMPANION(S)

MODE OF TRANSPORTATION

WEATHER

LODGINGS

LOCAL Cuisine

Best state delicacy eaten _____

GETTING CULTURED

Museums or other points of interest visited

FIRST TIME?

Was this your first visit, or are you basically a local?

YES ☐ NO ☐

HAD TO SEE IT TO BELIEVE IT

Strangest tourist attraction visited _____

RATE THE STATE

☆☆☆☆☆

Rhode Island

— est. 1790 —

THE OCEAN STATE Rhode Island may be the smallest state, but it has over 400 miles of pristine coastline. From the mid-1800s to the early 1900s, some of America's wealthiest citizens built summer homes along chic Newport's soaring cliffs. The decadence of the time is illustrative of the "Gilded Age." Incredible views of the estates may be seen on Cliff Walk, a path overlooking the sea. Throughout Rhode Island you'll find a variety of idyllic beach towns, including Narragansett, which offers some of the best spots to catch waves at Narragansett Town Beach. The Port of Galilee in Narragansett is a popular fishing boat dock, and the village has many oceanfront restaurants serving seafood dishes like their famous clam cakes! This is also where you may catch a ride to explore Block Island on the Block Island Ferry.

STATE FACTS

State Capital: **Providence**
State Flower: **Violet**
State Bird: **Rhode Island Red Hen**
State Mammal: **Harbor Seal**

Providence

The capital city sits along the confluence of several rivers. Because these rivers wind through the city, gondola rides are a popular way to see downtown. For a few months each year, a special celebration called WaterFire is held a few times each month, usually on Saturdays, during which floating bonfires create a warm glow on the dark water. Another fun way to enjoy a day in Providence is a trip to Roger Williams Park. This expansive park features numerous lakes and ponds to be explored by taking out one of the swan paddleboats, as well as an attached zoo, home to over one hundred wildlife species, including zebras, sloths, and elephants. Carousel Village, also within the park, features a hand-carved, classic carousel.

Coastal Treasures

- ❏ Block Island Southeast Lighthouse
- ❏ Pomham Rocks Lighthouse
- ❏ Bowen's Wharf
- ❏ Rosecliff mansion in Newport
- ❏ The Towers and the Town Beach in Narragansett
- ❏ Watch Hill Beach in Westerly

Rhode Island

THE OCEAN STATE

PROVIDENCE

WARWICK

HOPE VALLEY

NEWPORT

RHODE ISLAND
SOUND

BLOCK ISLAND
SOUND

ATLANTIC
OCEAN

RHODE ISLAND

JUST THE FACTS

DATE(S)
VISITED

TRAVEL
COMPANION(S)

MODE OF
TRANSPORTATION

WEATHER

LODGINGS

LOCAL Cuisine

Best state delicacy eaten

FIRST TIME?

Was this your first visit, or are you basically a local?

YES ☐   NO ☐

HAD TO SEE IT TO BELIEVE IT

Strangest tourist attraction visited

GETTING CULTURED

Museums or other points of interest visited

RATE THE STATE

☆☆☆☆☆

Vermont

— est. 1791 —

THE GREEN MOUNTAIN STATE An outdoor haven, the Green Mountain National Forest spans over 400,000 acres in Vermont. Quaint towns dot the landscape, providing picturesque visions of cozy main streets and covered bridges set over gently rolling streams. It's no surprise that American artist Norman Rockwell called Vermont his home. His artwork is noted for its scenes of idyllic American life, and what better inspiration for this than to live in Vermont? Country stores and maple syrup-covered pancakes hot off the griddle bring you back to a time when life was enjoyed at a slower pace.

STATE FACTS

State Capital: **Montpelier**
State Flower: **Red Clover**
State Bird: **Hermit Thrush**
Popular Food: **Maple Syrup**

The Maple Tree Roots of Vermont
Large maple trees are abundant in Vermont, with hundreds of farms producing over half of our country's syrup. Native Americans were the first to tap into the maple tree and extract the sap for boiling. Modern technology now makes it a slightly easier process, but the same principles apply. Around late February, farmers tap the trees and then plug them with a tube. A spout drains the sap into a bucket, the flow increasing as the weather warms during the spring. Once the buckets are filled, the sap is then collected and melted in sugarhouses.

Smugglers Notch
In the Green Mountains, there is a narrow pass along Route 108 that has a long history of illegal smuggling. It was first used by the British to avoid the embargoes of the early 1800s and then again, a century later, by Americans during Prohibition. This neck of the woods holds many secrets and legends. Stowe and Smugglers' Notch Resort are year-round playgrounds near this road, but because of heavy snow, it's only accessible in the warmer months.

Walk Across a Lake!
The Island Line Rail Trail over Lake Champlain connects Burlington to South Hero on Grand Isle and was built on an old railway line.

Vermont's Best Stops
❑ The Original Vermont Country Store in Weston
❑ Ben & Jerry's Waterbury Factory
❑ Burlington's Church Street Marketplace

LAKE CHAMPLAIN

• BURLINGTON

MONTPELIER ★

Vermont
THE
GREEN MOUNTAIN STATE

GREEN MOUNTAINS

VERMONT

JUST THE FACTS

DATE(S) VISITED

TRAVEL COMPANION(S)

MODE OF TRANSPORTATION

WEATHER

LODGINGS

LOCAL *Cuisine*

Best state delicacy eaten _____

_____

_____

_____

_____

_____

GETTING CULTURED

Museums or other points of interest visited

_____

_____

_____

_____

_____

FIRST TIME?

Was this your first visit, or are you basically a local?

☐ YES ☐ NO

HAD TO SEE IT TO BELIEVE IT

Strangest tourist attraction visited _____

_____

_____

_____

_____

_____

_____

RATE THE STATE

☆ ☆ ☆ ☆ ☆

110

THE
MID-ATLANTIC

The Mid-Atlantic is where the United States' government began, after the signing of the Declaration of Independence in Philadelphia in 1776 declared American independence from Great Britain. Colonial and American Revolutionary history is widespread throughout these states. From the busy streets of New York City to the rural countryside of Pennsylvania and the iconic boardwalks of New Jersey, a trip to the Mid-Atlantic is full of incredible sites to explore.

Delaware

— est. 1787 —

THE FIRST STATE Delaware became the first state on
December 7, 1787. It didn't have a legislative building at the time,
so thirty delegates met a few days before at the Golden Fleece Tavern in Dover to discuss
the Constitution. It was here that they agreed to join the Union. Though the original
tavern was demolished in 1830, stop into the new Golden Fleece Tavern and raise a glass
to the Founding Fathers! The nearby Dover Green served as a town center and was also
the site of important political activities in early colonial America.

STATE FACTS

State Capital: **Dover**
State Flower: **Peach Blossom**
State Bird: **Blue Hen**
Popular Food: **Peach Pie**

Rehoboth Beach

The Rehoboth Beach Boardwalk is one
mile long and has been a seaside retreat
on the East Coast since the 1800s. This
enjoyable resort town is referred to as the
"Nation's Summer Capital" because of
its proximity to Washington, DC. There
are numerous restaurants that serve
delectable seafood in casual settings
overlooking the Atlantic Ocean.

The Mispillion Riverwalk

The quaint town of Milford is a haven
for nature and arts along the winding
Mispillion River. While paddleboats
are an enjoyable way to spend a calm
afternoon on the water, strolling the
Riverwalk leads you past downtown
Milford's charming cafes and specialty
shops. In honor of the town's
shipbuilding past, multiple four-foot
model yachts are displayed throughout
the area, each intricately hand-painted
by individual artists.

Delaware's Favorite Sandwich

Capriotti's created their signature "Bobbie"
sandwich at their original location in
Wilmington. If you've never tried one,
it's like having Thanksgiving dinner on a
hoagie—complete with turkey, cranberry
sauce, and stuffing.

There's More to Explore

- ❏ Brandywine Creek State Park
- ❏ Bethany Beach
- ❏ Historic New Castle
- ❏ Winterthur Museum, Garden & Library
- ❏ Bird-watch at Bombay Hook National
    Wildlife Refuge
- ❏ Fenwick Island

Delaware

THE FIRST STATE

WILMINGTON

DOVER

DELAWARE BAY

CAPE HENLOPEN

REHOBOTH BEACH

DELAWARE

JUST THE FACTS

DATE(S) VISITED

TRAVEL COMPANION(S)

MODE OF TRANSPORTATION

WEATHER

LODGINGS

LOCAL Cuisine

Best state delicacy eaten _____

_____

_____

_____

_____

FIRST TIME?

Was this your first visit, or are you basically a local?

☐ YES   ☐ NO

HAD TO SEE IT TO BELIEVE IT

Strangest tourist attraction visited _____

_____

_____

_____

_____

GETTING CULTURED

Museums or other points of interest visited

RATE THE STATE

☆ ☆ ☆ ☆ ☆

114

Maryland

— est. 1788 —

THE OLD LINE STATE During the War of 1812, Francis Scott Key wrote "The Star-Spangled Banner" from a ship on the Chesapeake Bay, anchored just off Baltimore. This poem would go on to be published in newspapers throughout Maryland and later became the National Anthem. Like most of the states in the Mid-Atlantic region, Maryland was instrumental to America's founding and remnants of the colonial period are intertwined with modern life.

STATE FACTS

State Capital: **Annapolis**
State Flower: **Black-eyed Susan**
State Bird: **Baltimore oriole**
Popular Food: **Blue Crab**

Annapolis

The Annapolis Historic District looks similar to how it did centuries ago, but it's not frozen in time. It continues to thrive with small businesses that have preserved and repurposed the colonial buildings. A variety of restaurants, pubs, and boutiques line Main Street, leading down to the Chesapeake Bay. Branded the "Sailing Capital of America," lively City Dock is oftentimes referred to as "Ego Alley" for the expensive yachts that drop anchor here from all over the world. The spirit of the sea in Annapolis is also influenced by the presence of the United States Naval Academy.

Baltimore Crab Houses

North of Annapolis, Baltimore is another fascinating seaport city and the most populated in the state. Renowned for its crab houses, seafood lovers can indulge in every type of crab cuisine! Steamed crab in a bucket is traditionally served by the dozen and includes a handy mallet to get right down to business cracking shells. Between the months of April and November, there are many crab festivals to celebrate the state's crustacean.

Poe's Baltimore

Edgar Allan Poe lived and died in Baltimore. His former home, located at 203 N. Amity Street, is now a National Historic Landmark and available to tour by reservation. The Baltimore Ravens football team was named after his chilling poem "The Raven."

Maryland Escapes

❏ Swallow Falls State Park
❏ Assateague Island
❏ Calvert Cliffs State Park

Maryland

THE OLD LINE STATE

DEEP CREEK LAKE

POTOMAC RIVER

BALTIMORE

WASHINGTON DC

ANNAPOLIS

CHESAPEAKE BAY

OCEAN CITY

ATLANTIC OCEAN

MARYLAND

JUST THE FACTS

DATE(S) VISITED

TRAVEL COMPANION(S)

MODE OF TRANSPORTATION

WEATHER

LODGINGS

LOCAL Cuisine

Best state delicacy eaten _____

GETTING CULTURED

Museums or other points of interest visited

FIRST TIME?

Was this your first visit, or are you basically a local?

YES ☐　　NO ☐

HAD TO SEE IT TO BELIEVE IT

Strangest tourist attraction visited _____

RATE THE STATE

☆☆☆☆☆

New Jersey

— est. 1787 —

THE GARDEN STATE Most of New Jersey's major cities are in the northeastern part of the state. This region is closely tied to New York City, with many commuting across the Hudson River by train to work in Manhattan. South of this metro area, the famed Jersey Shore extends for 130 miles along the Atlantic Coast. There are also thousands of farms and over twenty-five public gardens throughout the Garden State.

STATE FACTS

State Capital: **Trenton**
State Flower: **Violet**
State Bird: **Eastern Goldfinch**
State Mammal: **Horse**

The Jersey Shore

The Jersey Shore features eighteen boardwalks along the coast, making New Jersey the state with the most boardwalks in America. The Atlantic City Boardwalk was built in 1870 and is the oldest and longest boardwalk in the world. This is also where saltwater taffy was first made at a candy shop! It wasn't until the 1970s that casinos came to the boardwalk, adding another level of entertainment to the miles of restaurants, souvenir shops, and rides at the pier. For a bird's-eye view of the ocean and the action below, take a ride on the 227-foot-tall Observation Wheel, located on Steel Pier.

The Music of Asbury Park

Asbury Park is the musical soul of the Jersey Shore. Bruce Springsteen, local to the area, contributed to the town's music origins, with his debut album *Greetings from Asbury Park, N.J.* Playing small venues like the Stone Pony set the stage for Springsteen's career and for the overall music scene to follow. It's easy to find live music every day of the week at one of the several venues in town, such as the Wonder Bar, or at the boardwalk concerts on the beach.

New Jersey's Must-see Gardens

- ❑ Grounds for Sculpture in Hamilton
- ❑ The Presby Memorial Iris Gardens in Montclair
- ❑ The New Jersey Botanical Garden in Ringwood
- ❑ Greenwood Gardens in Short Hills

New Jersey

THE GARDEN STATE

DELAWARE RIVER

HUDSON RIVER

• NEWARK

• JERSEY CITY

NEW
BRUNSWICK

★ TRENTON

• CAMDEN

ATLANTIC
OCEAN

• ATLANTIC CITY

DELAWARE
BAY

• CAPE MAY

NEW JERSEY

JUST THE FACTS

DATE(S)
VISITED

TRAVEL
COMPANION(S)

MODE OF
TRANSPORTATION

WEATHER

LODGINGS

LOCAL *Cuisine*

Best state delicacy eaten _____

GETTING CULTURED

Museums or other points of interest visited

FIRST TIME?

Was this
your
first visit,
or
are you
basically
a local?

☐ YES   ☐ NO

HAD TO SEE IT TO BELIEVE IT

Strangest tourist
attraction visited _____

RATE THE STATE

☆ ☆ ☆ ☆ ☆

New York

— est. 1788 —

THE EMPIRE STATE Everything is bigger in New York—the towering Manhattan skyscrapers, the enormous wonder of Niagara Falls, and, most importantly, the big dreams of so many people who made it into the dynamic state it is today. The Statue of Liberty proudly stands on the Hudson River as a welcoming symbol of freedom and democracy. Throughout the world, this monument is etched into the very fabric of what makes America the "Land of Opportunity." Immigrants who came to New York throughout history brought with them pieces of culture from their homelands. Because of this, New York has a spirit of new beginnings and remains a state of endless possibilities.

STATE FACTS

State Capital: **Albany**
State Flower: **Rose**
State Bird: **Eastern Bluebird**
Popular Food: **Pizza**

New York City
Anyone who has been to the "Big Apple" remembers the first time they were immersed in the energetic hustle of New York City. As the most populated city in the United States, it's loud, vibrant, and full of life, especially in Times Square. During the turn of the twentieth century, developers built upward, due to the lack of horizontal space, creating the iconic skyline. The Empire State Building was the first building in the world over one hundred stories tall. The copper spire at the top was intended to protect the building from lightning, and it works—it's struck multiple times every year during storms.

Did you know? America's first pizzeria, Lombardi's, was founded in 1905 in Little Italy.

Long Island
Though near New York City, Long Island is dramatically different, with sandy beaches, marshes, historic lighthouses, and old-fashioned windmills. One of the most renowned Long Island communities is the Hamptons, where many celebrities own luxurious summer homes. East of the Hamptons, the Montauk Point Lighthouse rests on a bluff overlooking the ocean, marking the furthest eastern point in the state. Drive across the island or take the Long Island Rail Road to many scenic destinations, including connections for ferries to Fire Island.

Beautiful Views in New York State
- ❏ Lake George
- ❏ Niagara Falls
- ❏ Ithaca
- ❏ The Hudson River Valley
- ❏ Fire Island

121

New York
THE EMPIRE STATE

LAKE CHAMPLAIN

LAKE ONTARIO

LAKE GEORGE

NIAGARA FALLS

ROCHESTER

SYRACUSE

UTICA

BUFFALO

LAKE ERIE

ITHACA

ALBANY ★

CATSKILL MOUNTAINS

HUDSON RIVER

DELAWARE RIVER

LONG ISLAND

FIRE ISLAND

NEW YORK CITY

ATLANTIC OCEAN

NEW YORK

JUST THE FACTS

DATE(S) VISITED

TRAVEL COMPANION(S)

MODE OF TRANSPORTATION

WEATHER

LODGINGS

LOCAL *Cuisine*

Best state delicacy eaten _____

_____
_____
_____
_____
_____

GETTING CULTURED

Museums or other points of interest visited

_____
_____
_____
_____
_____
_____

FIRST TIME?

Was this your first visit, or are you basically a local?

☐ YES   ☐ NO

HAD TO SEE IT TO BELIEVE IT

Strangest tourist attraction visited _____

_____
_____
_____
_____
_____
_____

RATE THE STATE

☆ ☆ ☆ ☆ ☆

Pennsylvania

— est. 1787 —

THE KEYSTONE STATE A keystone is architecturally the most important piece of a stone arch, inserted at the top to hold all the other stones together. Pennsylvania is this integral piece of American history, and geographically was the center of the thirteen original colonies. Pennsylvania also has gorgeous landscapes, with the Appalachian, Pocono, and Allegheny mountain ranges running through the state.

STATE FACTS

State Capital: **Harrisburg**
State Flower: **Mountain Laurel**
State Bird: **Ruffed Grouse**
Popular Food: **Philly Cheesesteak**

Philadelphia

One of the first sites to visit on a trip to Philadelphia is the Liberty Bell, on the grounds of Independence Hall. It's believed that this bell was first rung on July 8, 1776, four days after the adoption of the Declaration of Independence. Though there are many tales surrounding the 2,080-pound bell, the cause of its crack remains unknown. After sightseeing, grab a Philly cheesesteak for lunch. Local sandwich shops pride themselves on this Philadelphian-born sandwich and add their own twists to the classic version. Also visit the impressive Philadelphia Museum of Art, where Rocky Balboa ran to the top of the museum's front steps in the 1976 classic *Rocky*. The statue of Rocky on the grounds is a fun spot to take photos!

Sweet Hershey

Milton Hershey established the Hershey Chocolate Company in 1894. The community of Hershey grew from the original factory and today is a magical destination not only for indulging in Hershey's Kisses, but for an assortment of fun chocolatier attractions, including Hersheypark.

The Amish Villages of Lancaster County

There are miles of farmland across Lancaster County, often thought of as Dutch and Amish Country. This rural area has the largest Amish population in the United States. You'll spot white barns, windmills, and pastures, while the smell of fresh soil fills the senses. It's remarkable to be in a place where horses and buggies trot along unpaved roads and farmers utilize eighteenth-century plows. Prior to exploring the area, stop at the Amish Village to learn about their beliefs and way of life.

Key Stops in the Keystone State

- ❏ Gettysburg National Military Park
- ❏ Elfreth's Alley in Philadelphia
- ❏ The Andy Warhol Museum in Pittsburgh

LAKE ERIE

SCRANTON

DELAWARE RIVER

Pennsylvania

THE KEYSTONE STATE

PITTSBURGH

HARRISBURG

PHILADELPHIA

GETTYSBURG

PENNSYLVANIA

JUST THE FACTS

DATE(S)
VISITED

TRAVEL
COMPANION(S)

MODE OF
TRANSPORTATION

WEATHER

LODGINGS

LOCAL Cuisine

Best state delicacy eaten _____

GETTING CULTURED

Museums or other points of interest visited

FIRST TIME?

Was this your first visit, or are you basically a local?

YES ☐   NO ☐

HAD TO SEE IT TO BELIEVE IT

Strangest tourist attraction visited _____

RATE THE STATE

☆ ☆ ☆ ☆ ☆

THE
SOUTH

Stunning beaches, bayous, plains, and mountains make up the picturesque assortment of landscapes in the South. When traveling through the region, you're sure to find new terrains and experiences around every turn in the road. The origins of country, blues, and rock gives the southern states a musical history unlike anywhere in the country. It's also an area renowned for distinctive culinary flavors like barbecue, fried chicken, cornbread, and Cajun jambalaya. The South's history and diversity have led to some of the greatest contributions to music, food, and art in the United States.

Alabama

— est. 1819 —

THE YELLOWHAMMER STATE Alabama's nickname comes from their state bird, the Yellowhammer. These birds are instantly recognizable and may often be heard singing in the trees. There are stunning landscapes in Alabama, from the Appalachian Mountain foothills to the Gulf of Mexico's aqua waters. Mountains give way to fields of wildflowers in the valleys and cascading waterfalls are formed along the rivers. Because of its subtropical and humid climate, cotton grows well in the state.

STATE FACTS

State Capital: **Montgomery**
State Flower: **Camellia**
State Bird: **Yellowhammer**
Popular Food: **Shrimp and Grits**

Rocket City

Branded as "Rocket City," Huntsville has been synonymous with space exploration since the mid-twentieth century. The *Saturn V* rocket that propelled Neil Armstrong into space was developed by Huntsville engineers and is now on display at the US Space and Rocket Center. This otherworldly museum doesn't disappoint, with myriad rides, telescopes, and a spectacular planetarium. Ever dreamed of being an astronaut? Experience a virtual-reality space launch simulator or feel the weightlessness of being lifted 140 feet in the air on the Moon Shot.

Civil Rights History in Alabama

It's important to remember the wrongs of the past, to pursue a better future. Brave leaders like Dr. Martin Luther King, Jr. and Rosa Parks made fundamental contributions to civil rights in Alabama. One of the most impactful protests was led by Dr. King, marching from Selma to Montgomery and crossing the Edmund Pettus Bridge. This bridge will always symbolize the crossing over from oppression toward equality. Another critical moment leading to change occurred in 1955, when Rosa Parks defied the orders of a bus driver to move to the back of the bus in Montgomery. Her courage is revered at the Rosa Parks Museum, and the nearby Civil Rights Memorial Center features a striking memorial honoring those who gave their lives for equality and justice.

Did you know? There are more species of snail in Alabama than any other state!

Voyages on the Gulf

❏ Orange Beach
❏ Gulf Shores
❏ The Audubon Bird Sanctuary on Dauphin Island
❏ Gulf State Park

•HUNTSVILLE

BIRMINGHAM •

Alabama
THE
YELLOWHAMMER STATE

MONTGOMERY

•MOBILE

ALABAMA

JUST THE FACTS

DATE(S) VISITED

TRAVEL COMPANION(S)

MODE OF TRANSPORTATION

WEATHER

LODGINGS

LOCAL Cuisine

Best state delicacy eaten _____

_____

_____

_____

_____

_____

GETTING CULTURED

Museums or other points of interest visited

_____

_____

_____

_____

_____

_____

_____

FIRST TIME?

Was this your first visit, or are you basically a local?

☐ YES   ☐ NO

HAD TO SEE IT TO BELIEVE IT

Strangest tourist attraction visited _____

_____

_____

_____

_____

_____

_____

RATE THE STATE

☆ ☆ ☆ ☆ ☆

Arkansas

— est. 1836 —

THE NATURAL STATE Water is plentiful in the lakes, rivers, and bubbling hot springs of Arkansas. Mountain ranges span the state, wrapping around quaint towns. Because of its rare environment, Arkansas' soil is rich in minerals, including diamonds. The only diamond mine in the United States is located at Crater of Diamonds State Park, where visitors dig in the volcanic soil for diamonds and other gems. In fact, the country's largest diamond, fittingly nicknamed "Uncle Sam," came from this very mine!

STATE FACTS

State Capital: **Little Rock**
State Flower: **Apple Blossom**
State Bird: **Mockingbird**
Highest Mountain: **Mount Magazine**

Hot Springs

Nestled in the Ouachita Mountains, Hot Springs is renowned for its thermal pools. Native Americans bathed in the springs for thousands of years and considered the water to be healing. It wasn't until the early part of the nineteenth century that incoming settlers made it into a spa destination. Opulent bathhouses were constructed on Bathhouse Row, and tourism increased with America's curiosity in the health benefits. Two of the original bathhouses, the Quapaw and the Buckstaff, are available for soaking, and massages and other therapeutics are just as popular as the steaming mineral waters.

A Day in Little Rock

Little Rock is a vivacious capital city. You could spend hours in the River Market District, enjoying farmers' markets, restaurants, shops, and galleries while taking in the Arkansas River views. When you're ready to move on, hop on the Metro Streetcar, a trolley system that travels through the downtowns of both Little Rock and North Little Rock. There are many museums in the city, including the Old State House Museum, the Arkansas Museum of Fine Arts, and the Museum of Discovery.

A Beautiful Scenic Route

The Talimena National Scenic Byway crosses the mountain ranges between Arkansas and Oklahoma. This drive is remarkable for panoramic valley views and is especially exquisite in the fall. When heading west, this 54-mile drive begins in Mena, Arkansas, and ends in Talihina, Oklahoma.

Venturing Through Arkansas

❏ The Old Mill in Little Rock
❏ Artsy Eureka Springs
❏ Fort Smith National Historic Site
❏ Texarkana's State Line Post Office
❏ The Walmart Museum in Bentonville

131

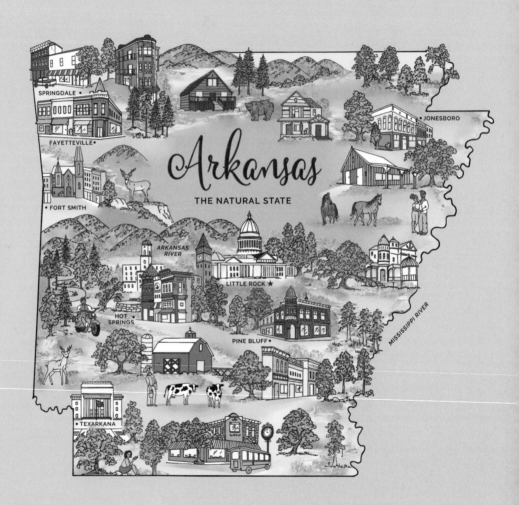

Arkansas

THE NATURAL STATE

SPRINGDALE •

FAYETTEVILLE•

• FORT SMITH

ARKANSAS
RIVER

HOT
SPRINGS

LITTLE ROCK ★

PINE BLUFF •

• TEXARKANA

• JONESBORO

MISSISSIPPI RIVER

ARKANSAS

JUST THE FACTS

DATE(S)
VISITED

TRAVEL
COMPANION(S)

MODE OF
TRANSPORTATION

WEATHER

LODGINGS

LOCAL Cuisine

Best state delicacy eaten _____

GETTING CULTURED

Museums or other points of interest visited

FIRST TIME?

Was this your first visit, or are you basically a local?

☐ YES ☐ NO

RATE THE STATE

HAD TO SEE IT TO BELIEVE IT

Strangest tourist attraction visited _____

Florida

— est. 1845 —

THE SUNSHINE STATE In 1513, Spanish conquistador Ponce de León set sail from Puerto Rico in search of the Fountain of Youth. He discovered Florida's coast instead. The Fountain of Youth Archaeological Park is supposedly the site of the fabled spring and visitors sip its water in hopes of receiving eternal youth. With its sun-kissed beaches and countless amusement parks, Florida is for all who are young at heart.

State Capital: **Tallahassee**
State Flower: **Orange Blossom**
State Bird: **Mockingbird**
State Reptile: **American Alligator**

Florida's Exciting Theme Parks

Orlando is the theme park capital of the world! Walt Disney World's Magic Kingdom is where dreams come true with Mickey and Minnie Mouse and all their friends. Universal Studios brings you into your favorite movies with rides inspired by *King Kong*, *Back to the Future*, the Harry Potter films, and more. SeaWorld takes you into underwater worlds with interactive experiences like the Shark Encounter tunnel.

Miami to Key West

Even during Florida's coldest months, the temperature usually hovers around seventy degrees. The beaches on the Atlantic Ocean offer more waves, while those on the Gulf of Mexico have calmer waters. South Beach in Miami has stunning white sands, suntanning beauties, glamor, and nightlife. There is a vivacious Cuban-American culture within the city and the neighborhood of Little Havana is famous for its incredible Cuban cuisine, such as the Cubano sandwich or a cup of café Cubano made with dark roasted espresso.

Farther south, an almost seven-mile-long causeway bridge over the ocean connects the mainland to Florida's magnificent Keys. While there are hundreds of keys and small communities within them, the main islands are connected by a chain of forty-two bridges. Once you reach the end of the line, you'll be at the most southern point of the continental United States. Known for Jimmy Buffett music and its Ernest Hemingway connections, Key West is the liveliest island in the Florida Keys.

Destinations for Days in the Sun
❏ Sanibel Island Seashells
❏ The Daytona International Speedway, Daytona Beach
❏ Everglades National Park
❏ The Kennedy Space Center
❏ Cocoa Beach
❏ Coral Gables' Venetian Pool

PENSACOLA •

TALLAHASSEE

• JACKSONVILLE

GAINESVILLE

DAYTONA

Florida

THE SUNSHINE STATE

ATLANTIC OCEAN

ORLANDO •

ST. PETERSBURG •

GULF OF MEXICO

CAPE CORAL •

MIAMI •

EVERGLADES •

THE KEYS

KEY WEST •

FLORIDA

JUST THE FACTS

DATE(S) VISITED

TRAVEL COMPANION(S)

MODE OF TRANSPORTATION

WEATHER

LODGINGS

LOCAL Cuisine

Best state delicacy eaten _____

GETTING CULTURED

Museums or other points of interest visited

FIRST TIME?

Was this your first visit, or are you basically a local?

☐ YES   ☐ NO

HAD TO SEE IT TO BELIEVE IT

Strangest tourist attraction visited _____

RATE THE STATE

☆☆☆☆☆

Georgia

— est. 1788 —

THE PEACH STATE We've all heard the phrase "sweet as a Georgia peach," and it's true: Georgia produces the tastiest peaches anywhere. During peach season, the juicy fruit are sold at roadside stands and served in all kinds of treats at festivals throughout the state. Beyond the peachy days of summer, there's so much to love about Georgia. For starters, the scenery is spectacular, from the coastal plains of the south to the Blue Ridge Mountains in the north. Even Atlanta has been coined as a "City in a Forest" due to the volume of trees in the metropolis. Life's simple things are enjoyed just a little bit more in Georgia, where having a glass of sweet tea on a patio swing may be the best way to spend some vacation time.

State Capital: **Atlanta**
State Flower: **Cherokee Rose**
State Bird: **Brown Thrasher**
Popular Food: **Peach Cobbler**

Charming Savannah
Located in Savannah's Historic District, Forsyth Park is the epitome of old-world charm. Since its founding in 1841, it's been an oasis of mossy oaks. The park's gorgeous fountain was added in 1858. As the oldest city in Georgia, there are moments you may feel as though you've stepped into the 1800s. Horse-drawn carriages trot down avenues of Victorian and colonial buildings and timeless streets await around every corner.

"Georgia on My Mind"
In Albany's Riverfront Park, legendary musician Ray Charles is memorialized in bronze atop a fountain. Wearing his iconic sunglasses and suit, he sits at his piano with his head tilted back mid-song. Piano keys surround the fountain where his statue slowly rotates. In the evening, the statue is illuminated and his songs are played as a free concert. A miniature version of his statue stands on a pedestal nearby, featuring a braille description for the blind and visually impaired.

View Seven States at Once!
Rock City's Lookout Mountain has views of seven states: Georgia, Alabama, Kentucky, North Carolina, South Carolina, Virginia, and Tennessee.

Wandering in Georgia
❏ Rome in the Appalachian Mountains
❏ The Atlanta Botanical Garden
❏ Augusta Riverwalk
❏ Wormsloe State Historic Site

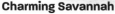

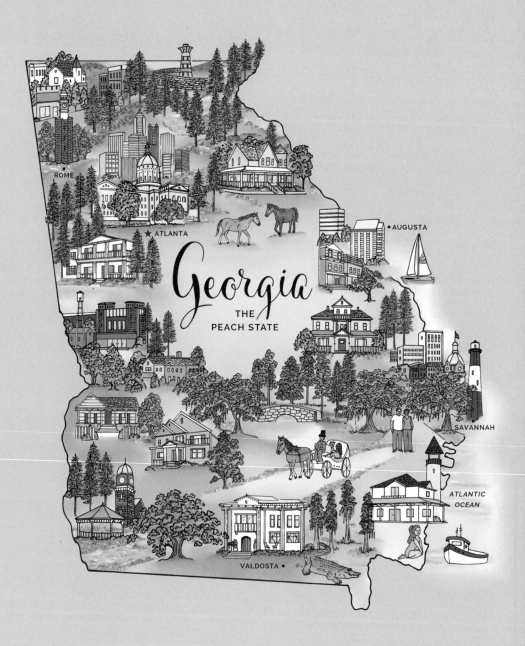

ROME

★ ATLANTA

• AUGUST A

Georgia

THE
PEACH STATE

SAVANNAH

ATLANTIC
OCEAN

VALDOSTA •

GEORGIA

JUST THE FACTS

DATE(S) VISITED

TRAVEL COMPANION(S)

MODE OF TRANSPORTATION

WEATHER

LODGINGS

LOCAL Cuisine

Best state delicacy eaten _____

_____

_____

_____

_____

_____

GETTING CULTURED

Museums or other points of interest visited

_____

_____

_____

_____

_____

FIRST TIME?

Was this your first visit, or are you basically a local?

☐ YES ☐ NO

HAD TO SEE IT TO BELIEVE IT

Strangest tourist attraction visited _____

_____

_____

_____

_____

_____

_____

RATE THE STATE

☆ ☆ ☆ ☆ ☆

Kentucky

— est. 1792 —

THE BLUEGRASS STATE Lexington is recognized for its hundreds of horse farms, where rolling hills divided by white fences and distinguished barns spread over the pastures, horses graze alongside their foals, and the grass has a tint of blueish-green. The soil in this region is rich in calcium, a byproduct of limestone under the surface, meaning the grass makes horses strong. Lexington's unofficial mascot, Big Lex, is a blue racehorse from the mid-nineteenth century who's said to have eaten too much of the bluegrass. Kentucky bluegrass is as much a part of the culture as it is a part of its ecosystem. Bluegrass music, for instance, originated in these hills.

State Capital: **Frankfort**
State Flower: **Goldenrod**
State Bird: **Northern Cardinal**
Popular Drink: **Mint Julep**

The Kentucky Derby in Louisville

Churchill Downs is the most acclaimed racetrack in America. In 1875, Meriwether Lewis Clark, Jr., a well-traveled man named after his famous grandfather, was inspired to bring the European style of horseracing to America. He built his dream in Louisville, along the Ohio River, and ever since, the annual "Run for the Roses" has captivated generations of fans. Traditions abound, including toasting mint juleps, wearing elaborate hats, and singing "My Old Kentucky Home." Though the Kentucky Derby only lasts for around two minutes, it's one of the most exciting two minutes in sports.

The *Belle of Louisville*

The *Belle of Louisville* is a National Historic Landmark. Built in 1914, she's still paddling down the Ohio River as the longest-operating steamboat in America. This Southern beauty has almost become a part of the river itself. There are several types of cruises on this icon, including special dinner cruises under starry skies with live music and dancing. Whatever the occasion, taking the riverboat ride is a delightful way to see Louisville's waterfront.

See a Moonbow

Located in the Daniel Boone National Forest, Cumberland Falls is one of only two places in the country to witness a moonlight rainbow, or "moonbow." (The other place to spot it is in California's Yosemite National Park.)

When Riding Through Kentucky

❏ Kentucky Bourbon Trail
❏ Kentucky Horse Park in Lexington
❏ The Country Music Highway, U.S. 23
❏ Sanders Café and Museum in Corbin

Kentucky

THE BLUEGRASS STATE

LOUISVILLE

OHIO RIVER

FRANKFORT

BOWLING GREEN

CUMBERLAND GAP

KENTUCKY

JUST THE FACTS

DATE(S) VISITED

TRAVEL COMPANION(S)

MODE OF TRANSPORTATION

WEATHER

LODGINGS

LOCAL *Cuisine*

Best state delicacy eaten _____

GETTING CULTURED

Museums or other points of interest visited

FIRST TIME?

Was this your first visit, or are you basically a local?

☐ YES   ☐ NO

HAD TO SEE IT TO BELIEVE IT

Strangest tourist attraction visited _____

RATE THE STATE

☆ ☆ ☆ ☆ ☆

Louisiana

— est. 1812 —

THE PELICAN STATE Louisiana's soulful character comes from its mysticism and multicultural heritage. Louisiana offers a kaleidoscope of travel experiences. On the streets of New Orleans and Baton Rouge, Mardi Gras parades pulsate with the rhythm of trombone players marching next to festive floats. The magic of Louisiana is also present in the subtle harmonies of nature; Spanish moss hangs from overgrown branches in the swamps and the melody of crickets singing under a full moon is always there, living in the stillness of the bayous.

STATE FACTS

State Capital: **Baton Rouge**
State Flower: **Magnolia**
State Bird: **Brown Pelican**
State Tree: **Bald Cypress**

New Orleans and the French Quarter

The French Quarter is the oldest neighborhood in New Orleans and has an eccentric history. Founded in 1718, the French strategically built the Old Square near the Mississippi River for trade purposes. As New Orleans grew into a major port city in the 1800s, Bourbon Street gained a reputation for its nightlife and vaudeville shows. In the centuries to follow, the area was influenced by people of many different nationalities and ethnicities, who brought their food, music, and religious beliefs with them. Voodoo customs, Mardi Gras celebrations, and lively burial ceremonies are all part of the city's mingled cultural traditions. Taste the culinary diversity in the spicy flavors of Cajun jambalaya and sweet French beignets.

Out on the Bayou

The bayous of Louisiana are gradually drifting water channels, composed of creeks, swamps, and marshes. The stagnant water and high humidity form ideal ecosystems for many species. Along with being a key habitat for alligators, turtles, snakes, and other exotic wildlife, birds also rely heavily on the bayou, so birdwatching is excellent. Blue herons, cranes, and pelicans graze the water's surface in search of food. Taking a boat tour through a swamp or bayou should be on your itinerary when visiting Louisiana, as you'll uncover new worlds you never knew existed.

Did you know? The Atchafalaya Swamp in Louisiana is the largest in the United States!

Beyond the Bayous

- ❑ New Orleans City Park
- ❑ Cathedral of St. John the Evangelist in Lafayette
- ❑ Baton Rouge
- ❑ Oak Alley Plantation in Vacherie

Louisiana

THE PELICAN STATE

SHREVEPORT

• ALEXANDRIA

MISSISSIPPI RIVER

LAKE CHARLES

LAFAYETTE

★ BATON ROUGE

• NEW ORLEANS

BRETON SOUND

GULF OF MEXICO

LOUISIANA

JUST THE FACTS

DATE(S)
VISITED

TRAVEL
COMPANION(S)

MODE OF
TRANSPORTATION

WEATHER

LODGINGS

LOCAL *Cuisine*

Best state delicacy eaten _____

_____

_____

_____

_____

FIRST TIME?

Was this your first visit, or are you basically a local?

☐ YES ☐ NO

HAD TO SEE IT TO BELIEVE IT

Strangest tourist attraction visited _____

_____

_____

_____

_____

_____

GETTING CULTURED

Museums or other points of interest visited

RATE THE STATE

☆ ☆ ☆ ☆ ☆

Mississippi

— est. 1817 —

THE MAGNOLIA STATE When standing on a bluff in Vicksburg, the mighty Mississippi River below is a spectacular sight. Countless stories are held in its slow-moving waters, as it flows south from its source in Minnesota. It's been the inspiration for numerous works of art and literature, like *Adventures of Huckleberry Finn* by Mark Twain. It's also the backdrop of much of America's history. Move slowly through the state, just like the river, to unveil the southern delights that make Mississippi unique.

STATE FACTS

State Capital: **Jackson**
State Flower: **Magnolia**
State Bird: **Mockingbird**
State Dance: **Square Dancing**

The Delta Blues

As legend has it, on a dark night at the intersection of two lonely highways in Clarksdale, a spirit appeared and taught the legendary musician, Robert Johnson, how to play a mean guitar in exchange for his soul. The story of the crossroads lives on somewhere between myth and history, and the junction of Highways 61 and 49 is considered the birthplace of the blues. Out of this low, often flooded terrain in northwest Mississippi, a distinctive sound arose, characterized by somber lyrics matched with a sliding guitar technique. From weathered porches shaded by cypress trees came blues musicians Charley Patton, B. B. King, and Muddy Waters.

Biloxi

Biloxi, with its beaches and casinos, is the "Playground of the South." Prior to legalized gaming in 1990, the mafia operated underground nightlife businesses for years on the Biloxi strip. The bounty of fish, shrimp, and crab found in the Gulf of Mexico also made the city a seafood capital. The Maritime and Seafood Industry Museum offers cruises on replica oyster schooner boats, where you can get a taste of the life of a sailor.

Mighty Mississippi Journeys

❏ Tupelo, the birthplace of Elvis
❏ Southern charm in Oxford
❏ The Biloxi Lighthouse
❏ Downtown Hattiesburg

Mississippi

THE MAGNOLIA STATE

OXFORD •

• TUPELO

MISSISSIPPI RIVER

• VICKSBURG

★ JACKSON

MERIDIAN

• HATTIESBURG

BILOXI •

GULF OF MEXICO

MISSISSIPPI

JUST THE FACTS

DATE(S) VISITED

TRAVEL COMPANION(S)

MODE OF TRANSPORTATION

WEATHER

LODGINGS

LOCAL Cuisine

Best state delicacy eaten _____

GETTING CULTURED

Museums or other points of interest visited

FIRST TIME?

Was this your first visit, or are you basically a local?

☐ YES ☐ NO

HAD TO SEE IT TO BELIEVE IT

Strangest tourist attraction visited _____

RATE THE STATE

☆☆☆☆☆

North Carolina

— est. 1789 —

THE TAR HEEL STATE Pirates hiding treasures in the Outer Banks, mermaids swimming in the Cape Fear River, sightings of Bigfoot in the Appalachian Mountains— all are familiar tales of old in North Carolina. These mysteries rise from the interior woodlands and quiet marshes on the coast. There's much to be fascinated by in North Carolina, where imagination runs as free as its horses.

STATE FACTS

State Capital: **Raleigh**
State Flower: **Flowering Dogwood**
State Bird: **Cardinal**
State Mammal: **Gray Squirrel**

The Outer Banks

Off the coast of North Carolina, a strand of barrier islands extends for 200 miles, where small communities live harmoniously with the sea and wildlife. In this restful oasis, time moves at the pace of the tides. Wild mustangs were brought to the Outer Banks by the Spanish on ships during the 1500s. The descendants of these horses now wander the shorelines of Corolla, Carova, and Currituck, and several wildlife sanctuaries in the Outer Banks protect the horses and native wildlife. For an unsurpassed view of the sea, climb the spiral staircase to the beacon of the Cape Hatteras Lighthouse. At 198 feet tall, it is the tallest lighthouse in America.

Captivating Asheville

Located in the foothills of the Blue Ridge Mountains, Asheville is a favored retreat in North Carolina. In the 1800s, the railroad turned Asheville into a mountain getaway, attracted artists, explorers, and even the tycoon George W. Vanderbilt. Vanderbilt purchased a large tract of land to build the opulent Biltmore Estate, which reflects Gilded Age wealth and glamour. There are 250 rooms and acres of spectacular gardens set amidst the trees. Afterward, relax at the adjoining Antler Hill Village, which has dining options and a winery.

Places of Wonder

- ❏ Sliding Rock in Pisgah National Forest
- ❏ Chimney Rock State Park
- ❏ North Carolina Museum of Natural Sciences in Raleigh
- ❏ Wilmington Riverwalk
- ❏ Mystery Hill in Blowing Rock

THE GREAT SMOKY MOUNTAINS

WINSTON - SALEM

• CHARLOTTE

★ RALEIGH

• GREENVILLE

FAYETTEVILLE

CAPE HATTERAS

WILMINGTON

ATLANTIC OCEAN

North Carolina

THE TAR HEEL STATE

NORTH CAROLINA

JUST THE FACTS

DATE(S) VISITED

TRAVEL COMPANION(S)

MODE OF TRANSPORTATION

WEATHER

LODGINGS

LOCAL Cuisine

Best state delicacy eaten _____

GETTING CULTURED

Museums or other points of interest visited

FIRST TIME?

Was this your first visit, or are you basically a local?

☐ YES ☐ NO

HAD TO SEE IT TO BELIEVE IT

Strangest tourist attraction visited _____

RATE THE STATE

☆ ☆ ☆ ☆ ☆

South Carolina

— est. 1788 —

THE PALMETTO STATE Whether you seek crisp mountain air, lounging on beaches under palmettos, or infinite entertainment in the cities, South Carolina offers the best of all worlds. Nature and urban life merge seamlessly in the capital city of Columbia, where three rivers can be found in its center. A trip through South Carolina will keep you wandering a little further than expected, to discover more than you imagined.

STATE FACTS

State Capital: **Columbia**
State Flower: **Yellow Jessamine**
State Bird: **Carolina Wren**
Popular Food: **Coconut Cake**

Myrtle Beach

When you're in the mood for a fun-filled oceanside getaway, look no further than Myrtle Beach. The temperature rarely climbs over eighty degrees and the water is warm enough to splash in the waves. You're sure to find the perfect spot to plant your toes in the sand, as this beach stretches for miles, and you can eat as much shrimp, crab, and oysters as possible at one of the multiple seafood buffets. With amusement parks, restaurants, and resorts situated right on the boardwalk, you'll never need to take off your flip-flops.

Charming Charleston

Pineapples were once a luxury fruit, imported from South America and brought to Charleston during the colonial era. They became an expensive delicacy, so offering a pineapple was a way to welcome important guests. At Charleston's serene Waterfront Park, the Pineapple Fountain overlooks Charleston Harbor as pelicans keep a watchful eye on the ships, and the fragrance of jasmine lingers in the breeze. Rainbow Row, a collection of eighteenth-century row homes in every shade of the color wheel along East Bay Street, sets the city's Antebellum architecture apart. The cheerful tones carry throughout downtown, including the shopping and dining hubs on King and Church Streets. Palms stand alongside oak trees, further blending a tropical feel with the traditional South.

The Angel Oak

Angel Oak on Johns Island in Charleston, is 65 feet high and some of its branches extend to over 100 feet in length. This living marvel has stood for centuries, a silent witness to history and all those who have rested under its canopy.

Inland Locations to See

- ❏ Swan Lake Iris Gardens in Sumter
- ❏ Falls Park on the Reedy River in Greenville
- ❏ Equestrian Life in Aiken
- ❏ Riverbanks Zoo & Garden in Columbia

GREENVILLE

SAVANNAH RIVER

★ COLUMBIA

FLORENCE

• AIKEN

LAKE
MARION

• MYRTLE BEACH

ATLANTIC
OCEAN

• CHARLESTON

South
Carolina

THE PALMETTO STATE

• HILTON HEAD
ISLAND

SOUTH CAROLINA

JUST THE FACTS

DATE(S)
VISITED

TRAVEL
COMPANION(S)

MODE OF
TRANSPORTATION

WEATHER

LODGINGS

LOCAL *Cuisine*

Best state delicacy eaten _____

_____

_____

_____

_____

FIRST TIME?

Was this your first visit, or are you basically a local?

☐ YES ☐ NO

HAD TO SEE IT TO BELIEVE IT

Strangest tourist attraction visited _____

_____

_____

_____

_____

GETTING CULTURED

Museums or other points of interest visited

RATE THE STATE

☆ ☆ ☆ ☆ ☆

Tennessee

— est. 1796 —

THE VOLUNTEER STATE Like the country songs written here, Tennessee is a melody of misty mornings in the Smoky Mountains, the twang of honky-tonks in Nashville, and banjos strumming in the hills. It's a musical state, where country and western music, rock and roll, and the blues all took shape, creating an ever-present harmony of life.

STATE FACTS

State Capital: **Nashville**
State Flower: **Iris**
State Bird: **Mockingbird**
State Gem: **Pearl**

Nashville's Country Music

Nashville is America's Music City. The Ryman Auditorium, opened in 1892, was meant to serve as a gospel tabernacle, but became a country icon in 1943, when the *Grand Ole Opry* moved in. Country music stars like Hank Williams, Patsy Cline, Loretta Lynn, Johnny Cash, June Carter, Tammy Wynette, and Dolly Parton have all performed on the Ryman stage. Spurred by the popularity of the show, recording studios were built on what is now Nashville's Music Row. Honky Tonk Highway, a street of neon-lit bars, was established shortly after, just around the corner.

Memphis and Elvis

Memphis is situated in the far southwest corner of Tennessee, near the Mississippi River. In the 1950s, entrepreneur Sam Phillips opened Sun Records there on Union Avenue, offering almost anyone with a guitar the opportunity to make their own record.

Elvis Presley eventually walked through the door and history was made. Phillips also discovered the talents of Johnny Cash, Jerry Lee Lewis, and B.B. King, among others. Elvis later purchased Graceland in Memphis, complete with iron gates adorned with music notes and the infamous "Jungle Room."

Great Smoky Mountains National Park

The Cherokee people referred to the Smoky Mountains as the "Land of Blue Smoke," alluding to the manifestation of a blueish smokey appearance hanging low between the mountains. During the June mating season, synchronous fireflies emit light in unison, creating a spectacle in the night sky.

Traveling Tennessee

❏ Gatlinburg, the "Gateway to the Smoky Mountains"
❏ The Johnny Cash Museum in Nashville
❏ Beale Street in Memphis
❏ Dolly Parton's Dollywood
❏ Chattanooga
❏ Knoxville

TENNESSEE

JUST THE FACTS

DATE(S)
VISITED

TRAVEL
COMPANION(S)

MODE OF
TRANSPORTATION

WEATHER

LODGINGS

LOCAL Cuisine

Best state delicacy eaten _____

GETTING CULTURED

Museums or other points of interest visited

FIRST TIME?

Was this
your
first visit,
or
are you
basically
a local?

YES   NO

HAD TO SEE IT TO BELIEVE IT

Strangest tourist
attraction visited

RATE THE
STATE

157

Virginia

— est. 1788 —

THE OLD DOMINION STATE History comes alive in Virginia, from the presidential homes of George Washington and Thomas Jefferson to the early settlements of Colonial Williamsburg and Jamestown. The far northeastern segment of the state sits on the Potomac River, with the city of Arlington directly across from Washington, DC. Many national monuments are in Virginia, including Arlington National Cemetery's Tomb of the Unknown Soldier and the US Marine Corps War Memorial. Potomac Park features striking views of the Washington Monument. In the capital city of Richmond, St. John's Church was where Patrick Henry ignited the flame of the Revolutionary War with his words, "Give me liberty, or give me death!"

STATE FACTS

State Capital: **Richmond**
State Flower: **American Dogwood**
State Bird: **Northern Cardinal**
Tallest Mountain: **Mount Rogers**

Colonial Williamsburg

During the eighteenth century, Williamsburg was the center of politics in Virginia and a very populated colony. The Colonial Williamsburg historic area is 301 acres of preserved, refurbished, and recrafted buildings. Walking through town, actors reenact scenes of colonial life while dressed in authentic period costumes. Horse-drawn carriages driven by coachmen offer a leisurely ride through the district. There is no better place to experience the daily life of the early colonists than Market Square, and the nearby Play House Stage offers outdoor entertainment in dramatic colonial style.

George Washington's Mount Vernon

George Washington's former estate brings you into his world in a more personal

way. Explore the mansion on a guided tour or take part in a longer specialty tour on topics ranging from the gardens and grounds to the lives of enslaved people who lived and worked at Mount Vernon. Washington's final resting place is also on the property, next to that of his wife, Martha. Every day, a wreath-laying ceremony takes place to pay respect to them.

Virginia is for (History and Nature) Lovers

- ❏ St. John's Church in Richmond
- ❏ Thomas Jefferson's Monticello
- ❏ Natural Bridge State Park
- ❏ Jamestown Settlement
- ❏ *King Neptune* statue in Neptune's Park, Virginia Beach

Virginia

THE OLD DOMINION STATE

HARRISONBURG

• ALEXANDRIA

POTOMAC RIVER

RICHMOND ★

WILLIAMSBURG

• VIRGINIA BEACH

VIRGINIA

JUST THE FACTS

DATE(S)
VISITED

TRAVEL
COMPANION(S)

MODE OF
TRANSPORTATION

WEATHER

LODGINGS

LOCAL Cuisine

Best state delicacy eaten _____

GETTING CULTURED

Museums or other points of interest visited

FIRST TIME?

Was this your first visit, or are you basically a local?

YES ☐   NO ☐

RATE THE STATE

★ ★ ★ ★ ★

HAD TO SEE IT TO BELIEVE IT

Strangest tourist attraction visited _____

West Virginia

— est. 1863 —

THE MOUNTAIN STATE West Virginia has a lot of country roads leading through small towns within deep "hollers" between the Appalachian Mountain ranges. The prevalence of naturally occurring coal within the mountains' crust has made the state a mining capital for generations. Thousands of miners have ridden into the darkness of the coal mines to work, and mining has become a significant part of the state's history.

STATE FACTS

State Capital: **Charleston**
State Flower: **Rhododendron**
State Bird: **Northern Cardinal**
Deepest Gorge: **New River Gorge**

The New River Gorge Bridge

The New River Gorge Bridge stretches 3,030 feet across the gorge that gave it its name, making it the longest single-span steel arch bridge in the United States. It stands 876 feet above the river below. To put the height into perspective, that's approximately 200 feet taller than both the Space Needle and Gateway Arch. When it opened in 1977, it helped residents immensely by connecting towns across the gorge. The bridge is honored at Bridge Day, which occurs annually on the third Saturday in October. This celebration is also known for extreme sports like zip-lining and parasailing. While driving across the bridge is common, walking across is only allowed on Bridge Day!

Harpers Ferry

Located at the confluence of the Shenandoah and Potomac Rivers, on a once-popular trade route, Harpers Ferry is an image of early America. Its location in the Blue Ridge Mountains lies where the borders of West Virginia, Virginia, and Maryland meet. Most of the town dates back over 200 years, including the original Harper House mansion, built by Harpers Ferry's founder. During the Civil War, an important battle took place here and destroyed some of the buildings (they've since been reconstructed). For history buffs, Harpers Ferry is a time capsule, with much of the town maintained as both a National Historic Park and Historic District.

A Country Road Scenic Drive

Route 60—the Midland Trail National Scenic Byway—travels across the state from Kenova to White Sulphur Springs. In between, this byway goes through Charleston and hugs the Kanawha River. By taking this road, you'll see West Virginia's versatility, from the state capital to the serenity of its mountain towns.

Country Road Travels

- ❏ Blackwater Falls State Park
- ❏ Riverton's Seneca Caverns
- ❏ Prabhupada's Palace of Gold in Moundsville
- ❏ Cass Scenic Railroad State Park

West Virginia

THE MOUNTAIN STATE

OHIO RIVER

POTOMAC RIVER

MORGANTOWN

PARKERSBURG

HUNTINGTON

CHARLESTON

SUMMERSVILLE

WELCH

WEST VIRGINIA

JUST THE FACTS

DATE(S) VISITED

TRAVEL COMPANION(S)

MODE OF TRANSPORTATION

WEATHER

LODGINGS

LOCAL Cuisine

Best state delicacy eaten _____

GETTING CULTURED

Museums or other points of interest visited

FIRST TIME?

Was this your first visit, or are you basically a local?

☐ YES   ☐ NO

HAD TO SEE IT TO BELIEVE IT

Strangest tourist attraction visited _____

RATE THE STATE

☆☆☆☆☆

163

FURTHER
JOURNEYS

Though they aren't states, two places you can't miss on your journey are Puerto Rico and Washington, DC. Puerto Rico, located in the Caribbean, is fairly close to the continental United States, making it easy to travel to the island. The capital city, San Juan, is the oldest city within the United States territories and was founded in 1519. If you're looking for a getaway to a tropical paradise, Puerto Rico is a spectacular island destination. Washington, DC, is a compact city, with countless monuments, memorials, museums, and historical sites to explore. Viewing the White House and the Capitol Building bring you to the heart of not only our nation's government, but of what these buildings represent to our people.

Puerto Rico

— United States Territory, est. 1898 —

THE ISLAND OF ENCHANTMENT Puerto Rico, a beautiful island located between the Caribbean Sea and the Atlantic Ocean, has pristine coastlines and a spirited society. Radiant colors give homes and buildings character, while architecture from the Spanish colonial period displays Puerto Rico's proud heritage. The El Yunque National Forest in the northeastern part of the island contains a wild ecological sphere within the rainforest's thick awning. Of all the diverse wildlife, the loudest is often the tiny male Coquí frog. They are found not only in El Yunque, but throughout Puerto Rico, and their calls into the night are a familiar song on the island.

Old San Juan

The capital of Puerto Rico, San Juan, is the most populated city on the island. Well away from the high-rises in San Juan's downtown, Old San Juan lies on an offshore island that is connected to the mainland by bridges. Standing over the bay is Castillo San Felipe del Morro, a Spanish fortress built in the late eighteenth century. Throughout Old San Juan, there are a total of three historical forts to explore. San Juan's history is intricately woven through time and place. As you walk down rows of colorful buildings, along cobblestone lanes, and under Fortaleza Street's vibrant umbrellas, the essence of this timeless city comes into full view.

Did you know? **Puerto Rico's large production of rum comes from the island's sugarcane fields. The first piña colada originated in San Juan.**

Beautiful Places to See

- ❑ Culebra and Vieques islands
- ❑ Catedral de San Juan Bautista in Old San Juan
- ❑ Mar Chiquita Beach Limestone Pool
- ❑ Plaza Las Delicias in Ponce
- ❑ Domes Beach in Rincón
- ❑ Mameyes Beach in Luquillo

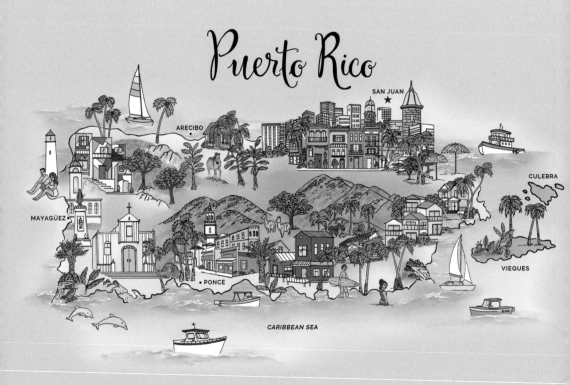

Puerto Rico

ARECIBO

SAN JUAN ★

CULEBRA

MAYAGÜEZ

VIEQUES

• PONCE

CARIBBEAN SEA

PUERTO RICO

JUST THE FACTS

DATE(S)
VISITED

TRAVEL
COMPANION(S)

MODE OF
TRANSPORTATION

WEATHER

LODGINGS

LOCAL *Cuisine*

Best state delicacy eaten _____

FIRST TIME?

Was this your first visit, or are you basically a local?

☐ YES   ☐ NO

HAD TO SEE IT TO BELIEVE IT

Strangest tourist attraction visited _____

GETTING CULTURED

Museums or other points of interest visited

RATE THE STATE

☆ ☆ ☆ ☆ ☆

Washington, DC

— est. 1790 —

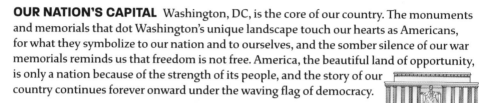

OUR NATION'S CAPITAL Washington, DC, is the core of our country. The monuments and memorials that dot Washington's unique landscape touch our hearts as Americans, for what they symbolize to our nation and to ourselves, and the somber silence of our war memorials reminds us that freedom is not free. America, the beautiful land of opportunity, is only a nation because of the strength of its people, and the story of our country continues forever onward under the waving flag of democracy.

The White House and the Capitol Building

The White House and the Capitol Building are usually the first stops when visiting Washington. Tours of the Capitol Building are available through the United States Capitol Visitor Center, leading visitors through the stunning Rotunda and National Statuary Hall. The Rotunda is an architectural masterpiece, with beautiful paintings adorning the walls and dome. Tours of the White House require advanced planning and are available by reservation only, but it may best be viewed outside from Lafayette Square.

Some Monuments and Memorials to Visit

- ❑ The Washington Monument
- ❑ The World War II Memorial
- ❑ The Martin Luther King, Jr. Memorial
- ❑ The Lincoln Memorial
- ❑ The Jefferson Memorial
- ❑ The Vietnam Veterans Memorial
- ❑ The Franklin Delano Roosevelt Memorial
- ❑ The Korean War Veterans Memorial
- ❑ The Ulysses S. Grant Memorial

- ❑ Theodore Roosevelt Island
- ❑ The African American Civil War Memorial
- ❑ The Albert Einstein Memorial
- ❑ The Dwight D. Eisenhower Memorial

Neighborhoods and Culture in Washington, DC

The National Mall, along Independence Avenue, is where you'll find several monuments, memorials, and museums, such as the Smithsonian National Museum of Natural History and the National Gallery of Art. To the east, Capitol Hill is the location of the United States Capitol, Library of Congress, and the Supreme Court. Exploring these areas alone could take several days, but Washington, DC, also has a wide assortment of eclectic neighborhoods to see. Historic Georgetown offers many delicious restaurants and interesting shops along the C&O Canal, while the vibrant Adams Morgan neighborhood is one of the most culturally diverse, known for its international cuisines and art from around the world!

168

Washington, DC

VIETNAM WAR
MEMORIAL

THE
WHITE HOUSE

SMITHSONIAN
MUSEUM

UNITED STATES
CAPITOL

LINCOLN MEMORIAL

WORLD WAR II
MEMORIAL

SMITHSONIAN
CASTLE

NATIONAL
GALLERY

NATIONAL MALL

WASHINGTON
MONUMENT

ULYSSES S.
GRANT
MEMORIAL

KOREAN WAR
MEMORIAL

MARTIN LUTHER
KING, JR.
MEMORIAL

TIDAL BASIN

THE WHARF

UNITED STATES
BOTANIC
GARDEN

FRANKLIN DELANO
ROOSEVELT
MEMORIAL

THOMAS JEFFERSON
MEMORIAL

POTOMAC
RIVER

WASHINGTON, DC

JUST THE FACTS

DATE(S) VISITED

TRAVEL COMPANION(S)

MODE OF TRANSPORTATION

WEATHER

LODGINGS

LOCAL Cuisine

Best state delicacy eaten _____

GETTING CULTURED

Museums or other points of interest visited

FIRST TIME?

Was this your first visit, or are you basically a local?

☐ YES ☐ NO

HAD TO SEE IT TO BELIEVE IT

Strangest tourist attraction visited _____

RATE THE STATE

★ ★ ★ ★ ★

Looking Back

When your journey is done, use these journaling pages to reflect on some of your favorite experiences and best memories!

TOP 5 FAVORITE STATES

1. ....
2. ....
3. ....
4. ....
5. ....

BEST FOODS I ATE

1. ....
....
2. ....
....
3. ....
....
4. ....
....
5. ....
....

BEST VIEWS

1. ....

2. ....

3. ....

4. ....

5. ....

BEST PLACES FOR OVERNIGHT STAYS

1. ....

2. ....

3. ....

4. ....

5. ....

MY LONGEST TRIPS

1. ....

2. ....

3. ....

4. ....

5. ....

BEST EVENTS I ATTENDED

1. ....

2. ....

3. ....

4. ....

5. ....

MY FAVORITE MEMORIES

Acknowledgments

I dedicate this book to my mom, Betty Stone, for her love and encouragement. I would also like to acknowledge my family and friends for supporting my artistic endeavors along the way. To my husband, Chad Laughlin: This is is for the many roads we've traveled together and for all of the adventures ahead of us.

It's with deep appreciation that I thank Lori Burke, Katie McGuire, and the Quarto team for making this book possible.

About the Author & Illustrator

Jessica Laughlin is an artist, graphic designer, photographer, and real estate agent. She is from Las Vegas, Nevada, where she graduated from the Las Vegas Academy of the Arts. She received her bachelor's degree from California State University Monterey Bay. Jessica lives in Henderson, Nevada, with her husband, Chad, and their dog, Gracie. She enjoys road trips, exploring the country, and creating art.

First published in 2024 by Epic Ink, an imprint of The Quarto Group,
142 West 36th Street, 4th Floor, New York, NY 10018, USA
(212) 779-4972 www.Quarto.com

Epic Ink titles are also available at discount for retail,
wholesale, promotional, and bulk purchase. For details, contact the
Special Sales Manager by email at specialsales@quarto.com or by mail
at The Quarto Group, Attn: Special Sales Manager,
100 Cummings Center Suite 265D, Beverly, MA 01915 USA.

10 9 8 7 6 5 4 3 2 1

ISBN: 978-0-76038-849-5

Group Publisher: Rage Kindelsperger
Editorial Director: Lori Burke
Creative Director: Laura Drew
Managing Editor: Cara Donaldson
Editor: Katie McGuire
Cover and Interior Design: Brad Norr Design

Printed in China